Robert L Ottley

The Hebrew Prophets

Robert L Ottley

The Hebrew Prophets

ISBN/EAN: 9783337037468

Printed in Europe, USA, Canada, Australia, Japan

Cover: Foto ©Lupo / pixelio.de

More available books at **www.hansebooks.com**

𝔒𝔯𝔣𝔬𝔯𝔡 𝔆𝔥𝔲𝔯𝔠𝔥 𝔗𝔢𝔯𝔱 𝔅𝔬𝔬𝔨𝔰

The Hebrew Prophets

BY

THE REV. R. L. OTTLEY, M.A.

RECTOR OF WINTERBOURNE BASSETT, FORMERLY PRINCIPAL
OF PUSEY HOUSE, OXFORD, AND BAMPTON LECTURER

RIVINGTONS
KING STREET, COVENT GARDEN
LONDON
1898

CONTENTS

CHAP.		PAGE
I.	The Meaning, Origin, and Early History of Prophecy,	1
II.	The Prophets of the Eighth Century B.C.,	17
III.	Prophecy in the Seventh Century B.C.,	44
IV.	The Prophets of the Exile,	62
V.	After the Exile,	78
VI.	Later Post-Exilic Prophecy,	91
VII.	The Messianic Hope	106
CHRONOLOGICAL TABLE,		119
INDEX,		123

THE HEBREW PROPHETS

CHAPTER I

THE MEANING, ORIGIN, AND EARLY HISTORY OF PROPHECY

'The Prophets' is the title given by the Jews to one section of their sacred Scriptures. The first division is called the Law (*Torah*), and consists of the five books of the Pentateuch; the second division is called the Prophets (*Nebiim*), and consists of two portions, (1) the former Prophets (*Nebiim Rishonim*), *i.e.* four historical books which were apparently compiled, and partly written, under the guiding influence of men endued with the prophetic gift: Joshua, Judges, and the books of Samuel and Kings.[1] (2) The latter Prophets (*Nebiim 'Acharonim*) are also reckoned as four books, *i.e.* three great prophets, Isaiah, Jeremiah, Ezekiel, and one book of minor prophets, sometimes called in Greek τὸ δωδεκαπρόφητον. The third division of the Hebrew Scriptures, called the Writings (*Kethubhim*, Greek ἁγιόγραφα), contains the remaining books of the Hebrew canon, some of which are poetical, *e.g.* the Psalms, Job, Lamentations, and the Song of Solomon; others historical, *e.g.* Chronicles, Ezra, Nehemiah; one only being prophetic in character, viz. the book of Daniel.

The former Prophets.—In this book we are only concerned with 'the prophets' and not with all of them, but only with the 'latter prophets.' It is, however, important to bear in mind the fact that some of the historical books are classed as 'prophets.' This fact is a proof that the books of Joshua, Judges, Samuel, and Kings are not

---

[1] The *four* books (1 and 2 Samuel, 1 and 2 Kings) formed in the Hebrew only two: the book of Samuel and the book of Kings.

mere annals or chronicles of Hebrew history. They contain history and something more. They *interpret* the events which they describe, and constantly draw attention to the purposes which Almighty God had in view throughout His dealings with the chosen people. The events recorded are selected and arranged in such a way as to illustrate the leading ideas of the prophetic writers, especially, perhaps, the thought of God's faithfulness to His covenant promises in spite of the oft-repeated rebellion and apostasy of His chosen people, the certainty and severity of His judgments, and the depth and constancy of His compassion.

Collection of the Prophetic Writings.—Various writings of the prophets, former and latter, were probably compiled or collected together shortly after the close of the exile, and they gradually came to be regarded as authoritative scripture, worthy of a place next to the sacred 'Law,' during the fifth century B.C. There is doubtless an element of truth in the tradition mentioned in 2 Macc. ii. 13, that Nehemiah founded a library and *gathered together the books concerning the kings and the prophets and the (books) of David and the letters of the kings about sacred gifts*. At any rate, we have good reason to believe, that in the days of Nehemiah's activity at Jerusalem (*circ.* 445-430), there arose a widespread desire to collect and preserve the sacred utterances of the Hebrew prophets; but it is most probable that even if the work of collecting the prophetic writings began in Nehemiah's time, the process of selection, compilation, and revision was not completed before the middle of the fourth century B.C. Indeed, there are indications that *the prophets* were not finally ranked as canonical scripture till nearly the close of the third century B.C.

The process of formation was thus a prolonged one, leaving ample time for the discovery and incorporation in the book of the prophets of various scattered fragments of prophecy. Occasionally these fragments were inserted among the authentic writings of some ancient prophet. For example, the prophecies of the great writer who is usually called 'the second Isaiah' (Isa. xl.-lxvi.), and possibly passages due to other unknown hands, seem certainly to have been included among the authentic writings of Isaiah; and there are strong reasons for supposing that other books, *e.g.* Micah and Zechariah, contain considerable portions which are not the work of their reputed authors. It is unlikely that any final collection of the prophetic writings took place until there arose among the Jews a consciousness that the gift of prophecy was withdrawn from Israel, and that it was important to collect all that the true spirit of prophecy had actually produced. The fact that the book of Daniel is not included among 'the prophets,' confirms the supposition that the compilation was virtually complete before the appearance of that book; the mention of Isaiah, Jeremiah, Ezekiel and 'the twelve prophets' in Ecclus. xlviii., xlix., seems to indicate that their writings were already well known in the form of a separate collection, about the year 180 B.C. It may be accordingly taken for granted that 'the prophets' assumed their final shape, and were generally recognised as canonical scripture some time before the close of the third century B.C.

The place of Prophecy in Israel's religion.—In this book we are concerned with the 'latter prophets,' and it will be well to begin by considering briefly, how large and important a part was played by prophecy in the gradual development and growth of Hebrew religion. The Bible describes most of the great servants of God, who were recipients of His promises, leaders of His people, founders of Israel's sacred institutions, or instruments of the divine will, as 'prophets.' For instance, the patriarch Abraham is called a prophet (Gen. xx. 7); Moses is more than once so described (Deut. xxxiv. 10, Hos. xii. 13); so also are Samuel (1 Sam. iii. 20), David, the royal psalmist of Israel (Acts ii. 30), and others who left behind them no writings, such as Elijah and Elisha. Jehovah had indeed promised that His people should never be left destitute of the guidance of a prophet, who should declare to them the divine will (see Deut. xviii. 15, etc.). Israel's religion was, in fact, a religion of *revelation*. The Hebrews firmly believed in a personal God, who was willing to make Himself known to man in ways adapted to human capacity. Thus, throughout the Bible, we read of God declaring His will to men by means of visions, dreams, oracles, angelic communications, or the direct utterances of inspired prophets. The devout Hebrew felt himself called to a life of true friendship or intimacy with God. He desired to know more of the gracious being who had done such great things for his forefathers; he eagerly awaited the declaration of God's will, and it seemed to him perfectly natural that God should have special instruments or messengers through whom His nature, His purposes, and His requirements of man were continuously revealed.

The word *Nabhi*.—The Hebrews had two different names for a prophet, one of which is much more rarely employed than the other. In 1 Sam. ix. 9, we read that a more ancient title than *prophet* (*Nabhi*) was *seer* (*Ro'eh* or *Chozeh*).[1] It may be that the change of name implies a change in the functions of the prophet; possibly it indicates a contrast between two different orders of men, or it may point to a difference of origin. The passage in 1 Sam. ix., however, implies no more than that the word *Ro'eh* was an early title which was afterwards superseded by the more familiar *Nabhi*. At any rate this latter word (plur. *Nebîim*) became the ordinary term employed to denote a prophet, and an inquiry into its meaning is essential if we are to get a true idea of what the Hebrews understood by prophecy. The Semitic root from which *Nabhi* is derived is found in the ancient language of Assyria and Babylonia, and also in Arabic. In the Assyrian dialect it has the simple meaning 'utter' or 'proclaim.' It appears in such divine or royal titles as *Nebo* or *Nabu*, *Nebu-kadnezar*, *Nabo-polassar*, etc. In Arabic, however, the root has a more clear and precise connotation; it implies the utterance of a message which the speaker is *commissioned* to deliver. *Nabhi* thus appears to have originally meant 'a *commissioned* speaker'; one who utters a message which he is commanded to deliver on behalf of another. Thus in Exod. vii. 1, Aaron is described as the 'prophet'

---

[1] *Ro'eh*, 1 Sam. ix. 11, 18, 19; 1 Chron. ix. 22; xxvi. 28, etc.; Isa. xxx. 10. *Chozeh*, 2 Sam. xxiv. 11, frequently in Chronicles and sometimes in the prophets.

of Moses because he speaks in the name and by the commission of Moses; and in Jer. xv. 19, Jehovah says to Jeremiah, *Thou shalt be as my mouth* (cp. i. 9).

The word 'prophet' then signifies 'an accredited messenger' of Almighty God, and accordingly the usual style of address in the older prophets is *Thus saith Jehovah*.[1] The prophet's message is authoritative as being *The word of Jehovah* to His people. His main function is to preach, to rebuke, to exhort, to proclaim Jehovah's will. In fact the title *Nabhi* did not suggest to a Hebrew mind the associations which we usually connect with the English word *prophet*. We are apt to think of *prediction* as the main element in a prophet's work. But this was by no means the Hebrew conception of the prophetic office. *Nabhi* means not so much one who *foretells the future*, as *a forthteller*: a proclaimer to men of a divine message.

The Prophet's function.—Prediction was by no means the chief part of a prophet's function. Even a superficial study of the writings of Isaiah or Micah will show us that the prophet was more of a preacher than a seer. He denounced the sins of his contemporaries; he proclaimed the righteous judgments of God; he rebuked in burning words the national sins by which Jehovah's name was dishonoured; he made it his business *to declare unto Jacob his transgression and to Israel his sin* (Micah iii. 8). The godlessness of statesmen, the heartless luxury of the rich, the formalism and hypocrisy of the priests, the greed and deceitfulness of false prophets,—these formed the theme of his utterances. And the Hebrew prophets differed from the ordinary soothsayers of heathendom, not only in the fact that they were fully conscious of a divine mission when they uttered their oracles, but also because they were above all things preachers of *righteousness*. They did not busy themselves with the dark secrets of the future;[2] they addressed themselves to the crying needs of the present. They laboured to turn sinners from their iniquity and to

---
[1] Lit. (*The*) *oracle of Jehovah*. See Professor Cheyne on Isa. i. 24.
[2] Consider Isa. viii. 19 ff. Cp. Deut. xviii. 10, 11.

bring them to repentance; they strove to keep alive in men's hearts *the light of the Lord* (Isa. ii. 5), *i.e.* the fear of Jehovah and the true knowledge of His law. And they well knew that they were enabled for their hard and high task by the Spirit of Jehovah Himself, and that He who bade them speak was present with them to strengthen and protect them according to their need (Jer. i. 8, 19).

Origins of Prophecy.—Such then was the Hebrew conception of a *Nabhi*, but we must not suppose that this sublime and simple idea of prophecy arose all at once. The prophetic gift as we see it fully manifested in holy men of God like Amos and Isaiah was a thing gradually developed from very lowly beginnings. An order of prophets was in fact an institution which Israel originally shared with the heathen inhabitants of Canaan and of the adjacent countries. The power of prophecy was closely connected with the tendency to a certain ecstatic religious fervour or excitement which is characteristic of the Semitic temperament, and which may be witnessed at this day in the wild behaviour of an Eastern dervish, or in the frenzied enthusiasm of the pilgrims at holy Mecca. The gods of Phœnicia had their prophets, and we read in the Old Testament itself of the 'prophets' of Baal—fanatical devotees who by wild dancing and music endeavoured to attract the attention of their god or to win his favour, mutilating themselves with knives and lancets and leaping on the altar (1 Kings xviii. 28). In many respects akin to these Canaanitish *Nebiim* seem to have been the companies of prophets of whom we read in the first book of Samuel. It is very possible that the strain and pressure of Philistine domination excited a strong outburst of patriotic enthusiasm on behalf of Jehovah's land and religion, of which one result was the choice of Saul as Israel's first king. Thus in 1 Sam. x. 5-13, xix. 23 ff., we read of *Nebiim* who seem to have lived together in schools or companies. Probably they wore a coarse garment of skin as a special mark of their religious calling, and they may have depended for support on the charity of pious Israelites, like the begging friars of mediæval times. But they do not appear to have been regarded with much reverence by the people in general. The prophet who was commissioned to anoint Jehu king, was contemptuously described as a 'mad fellow' (2 Kings ix. 11), and men were astonished that a warrior like Saul should be found in the strange company of *Nebiim* (1 Sam. x. 11, xix. 24). Even in such great men as Elijah and Elisha, the prophetic gift seems to have occasionally depended on certain physical conditions (1 Kings xviii. 46, 2 Kings iii. 15); but apparently these conditions accompanied only the earlier stages in the history of prophecy. In its perfect form prophetic enthusiasm was no mere involuntary ecstasy, but a supernatural exaltation of spirit, of which the prophet was himself fully conscious. It is important to recognise, in the history of prophecy, the principle which pervades Israel's entire religious development, Almighty God condescending, as it were, to use a defective and rudimentary institution—a rude native outgrowth of the Semitic character—as the basis or crude material out of which a high and sacred faculty was to be developed. The lowly elements which marked the beginnings of prophecy ultimately disappeared, and a comparison of its earliest with its latest stage aptly illustrates the profound maxim of St. Paul: *Howbeit that was not first which is spiritual, but that which is natural; and afterward that which is spiritual* (1 Cor. xv. 46).

The work of Samuel.—The work of **Samuel** in connection with prophecy seems to have been of peculiar importance. In Acts iii. 24, he is mentioned as a prominent figure in the line of prophets, and indeed as having practically inaugurated a new epoch in Israel's religion. His chosen task—one for which his own religious training had specially qualified him—was that of regulating and organising the turbulent and boisterous element in the behaviour and character of the *Nebiim* in order to enlist the prophetic gift in the service of a higher and purer type of religion. The 'schools of the prophets' formed by Samuel were probably designed to be a means of cherishing the prophetic gift, and of thereby rekindling the religious life of the people which, during the wild and lawless period of the judges, had fallen into decay. Accordingly we find Samuel gathering together in schools or companies those *Nebíim* who had hitherto been in the habit of traversing the land in wild and frenzied excitement, probably preaching a crusade against Philistine oppression, and endeavouring to enlist recruits on behalf of Israel's religion and territory.

The Schools of the Prophets.—We know very little of the schools of the prophets. It is probable that many of the *Nebíim* took the Nazirite vow, and led an ascetic life. Very possibly the art of music was cultivated among them, and they may even have formed a school of sacred literature in which the ancient traditions of Israel's past history were committed to writing, and fragments of early poetry and annals were collected. It is certain at any rate that henceforth the schools of the prophets occupied a recognised and important place among the religious institutions of Israel. We hear of them again in connection with the reign of Ahab, which, in consequence of the king's marriage with Jezebel, the daughter of the heathen king of Sidon, was a period of special peril to the interests of the true religion. Preeminent among the prophets of Ahab's time is of course the majestic figure of **Elijah**, whose life was devoted to the maintenance of Jehovah's religion against the worship of Baal. Elijah is in a sense the first of the prophets, and his career illustrates the immense influence of personality in the religious history of the Hebrews. Samuel's careful organisation of the *Nebíim* had doubtless effected much both for the political and religious interests of Israel. The *Nebíim* had doubtless inspired to a great extent the national movement which led to the foundation of the monarchy. As religious teachers they had probably come to occupy a place alongside of the priests, and already, as it seems, they were recognised as a religious order, 'sons of the prophets,' devoted to the work of inculcating and fostering the great religious truths which Israel held in trust for mankind. But the influence of the *Nebíim* was after all unequal to that of a single powerful leader like Elijah. They were faithful disciples and obedient instruments of greater men than themselves —men who acted on the life and thought of their age by the sheer force of inspired personality.

THE PROPHETS AND THE NATION

The Prophets and the Nation.—Elijah is the foremost of those great leaders of religion whom we call *par excellence* the Hebrew prophets. He 'introduced into prophecy,' it has been said, 'that species of categorical imperative which distinguishes him as well as the later prophets; that brazen inflexibility, that diamond-like hardness of character, which bids them hold fast by their moral demand even should the nation be dashed in pieces against it.'[1] Moreover, the active life of Elijah illustrates the extent to which the prophets made their influence felt in the nation's public life. They exercised their ministry in close relation to the political circumstances of their time. They have been truly called 'watchmen of the theocracy,' since they habitually followed with close interest the course of events, whether political or religious, and regarded it as their duty to intervene in public affairs from time to time in order to bring to the remembrance of their countrymen those fundamental religious truths on which the theocratic state was based, viz., that Jehovah alone was Israel's God, that Israel was His chosen people, and that His supreme requirement was the observance by the nation of the revealed law of righteousness. Thus they aimed at keeping Israel faithful to Jehovah, as He had manifested Himself at Sinai—as a God who delighted in pure worship, in righteous dealing, and in fraternal charity between man and man.

The Prophets and the Kings.—In an oriental state the influence and example of the ruler must always be of paramount importance. Consequently the prophets made it their special business to control and judge the conduct of the reigning monarch. Their reputation and position in the State might indeed vary from time to time in accordance with the character or caprices of a particular king. In the reign of David the office of prophet was exercised harmoniously with that of the monarch, since David himself had apparently from the first set before himself the true theocratic conception of kingship (cp. 2 Sam. xxiii. 1-7), and had himself before he came to

---

[1] Kittel, *History of the Hebrews*, vol. ii. p. 266.

the throne had close connections with the *Nebîim* (1 Sam. xix. 18). Prophets were held in honour by upright monarchs like Hezekiah and Josiah, but sooner or later their fearless denunciations of vice could scarcely fail to bring them into collision with royal self-will, or popular prejudice and fanaticism. Thus, one and all, they were called, each in greater or less degree, to suffer for their faith, for their boldness in rebuking sin, or for their devotion to the service of Jehovah. *Which of the prophets*, says St. Stephen, *have not your fathers persecuted? and they have slain them which showed before of the coming of the Just One* (Acts vii. 52, cp. Luke xi. 47, Matt. xxiii. 30). They suffered indeed not merely as public witnesses for God, but also as godly men who fulfilled their mission by their lives as well as by their preaching. For as 'men of God,' 'servants of Jehovah,' the prophets felt themselves called to a life of special intimacy with Jehovah. Indeed, the title 'servant of Jehovah' was in an ideal sense applicable to Israel as a people; but it also expressed the true vocation of each individual Israelite, since the fulfilment of Jehovah's purpose demanded a dispensation in which all should be prophets and all should know Jehovah, *from the least even to the greatest. Would God*, cried Moses, when Joshua envied for his sake, *that all the Lord's people were prophets, and that the Lord would put His Spirit upon them* (Num. xi. 29). The prophets, meanwhile, actually realised in their own persons the vocation which ideally belonged to Israel as a whole. Whether we think of the holiness of their own lives, of the closeness of their intimacy with God, or of the sorrows they were called to endure, we shall see that they typically represented the calling and function of the *righteous nation* (Isa. xxvi. 2) viewed in its entirety.

The Prophets and the Priests.—There was another class of persons with whom we find the prophets in frequent antagonism, viz., the priests of the various shrines at which the service of Jehovah was carried on. According to the intention of the earliest law-giver, the priests were to be the permanent religious teachers of the nation. They were to instruct the people on points of religious and moral duty, and in special cases of difficulty they were to impart *Torah*, i.e. oral instruction, which gradually assumed the shape of customary law and was ultimately embodied in a written code. But while the priests were permanent teachers of *Torah*, and ministers through whom the covenant people exercised its privilege of drawing near to Jehovah, the prophets were the occasional messengers through whom God drew near to His people and communicated to them His will. Generally speaking, the priests were ready to submit themselves to the prophets as extraordinary and direct agents of Jehovah; but naturally the *tendency* of the priesthood was to exaggerate the importance of their own functions, to make much of minor points of sacrificial ritual, or formal laws of ceremonial purity, and so in careful observance of details to lose sight of great moral and spiritual principles. The prophets, on the other hand, were chiefly concerned with the preaching of the moral law; and in placing morality on a higher level than ritual they undoubtedly continued and developed the original teaching of Moses himself. In the most ancient legislation (the Decalogue and the so-called 'Book of the Covenant'), the claims of mercy, justice, and good faith had occupied the most prominent place, and on these the prophets were continually insisting. They often speak in a depreciatory style of sacrifice, though they do not by any means reject it. What they insist upon is that punctiliousness in sacrifice is no equivalent for civil and social well-doing. They abhor the formal profession of religion when divorced from righteous conduct; they cannot tolerate the substitution of sacrifice, however costly and elaborate, for the fulfilment of ordinary moral duties. On the whole, the attitude of the prophets towards sacrifice is negative. They content themselves with condemning such elements in the popular *cultus* as are insulting or dishonouring to Jehovah, *e.g.* the use of images, or riotous excess in the sacrificial feasts; and they invariably exalt the fulfilment of moral duty above the external practices of religion. Their teaching may be illustrated by such typical passages as 1 Sam. xv. 22; Isa. i. 11-17; Amos v. 21, 22; Micah vi. 7; Jer. vi. 20, vii. 21-23.

We have already noticed the close relation in which prophecy stands to the general history of Israel. During the earlier period of the monarchy, however, prophecy took the form of an occasional rebuke fearlessly administered by individual men of God to unrighteous rulers. Thus, Samuel had rebuked Saul; Nathan and Gad had reproved David; and Elijah had denounced the crimes of Ahab. But with the appearance of the last-mentioned prophet a new epoch begins. Before the accession of Ahab, Israel had come into collision with the neighbouring kingdom of Syria, and had thus been drawn, as it were, on to the broad stage of secular history. It was a moment when Israel was in danger of utterly forgetting its peculiar calling. The weak indulgence with which Ahab treated his idolatrous queen did not indeed go to the length of formally extirpating the religion of Jehovah. We hear of about four hundred prophets of Jehovah. But Ahab, like Solomon, allowed his wife to introduce the worship of the Tyrian Baal, and to erect a sanctuary in his honour. There was acute danger of national apostasy from the religion of Jehovah. This is the point of Elijah's question, *How long halt ye between two opinions?* (1 Kings xviii. 21). In the worship of Baal the prophet discerned not so much a proof of the royal tolerance, as an act of disloyalty to the national Deity. Israel could not fulfil its true destiny so long as it wavered in its allegiance to Jehovah. Thus, in his denunciation of Ahab's personal crimes, Elijah was acting as the champion of religion itself.

Elisha, the disciple and successor of Elijah, was, like his master, a man of special spiritual gifts, and exercised a scarcely less powerful influence on his contemporaries, as is sufficiently proved by the multitude of miracles ascribed to him. Most significant, however, is the very decided part played by Elisha in the revolution which led to the downfall of Ahab's dynasty and raised Jehu to the throne of Israel. In his conduct at this crisis Elisha was resolutely carrying out the religious policy of his predecessor Elijah, whose constant aim had been the total extirpation of Baal-worship.

The career of the two great prophets just mentioned

illustrates very clearly the functions of a Hebrew prophet. As we have seen, a prophet was a man guided and inspired by God, and acting under commission from Him; a man who looked at contemporary history in the light of those great religious ideas which Moses had transmitted; a watchman who kept his eyes open for the signs of the times and who warned his countrymen of the impending judgments of God; an 'incarnate conscience' who perceived and presented in its true light all that was unjust or corrupt in the ordinary life and social arrangements of his time; who recognised in history, and specially in the disasters which befell his nation, the warnings and chastisements of Almighty God. Nor can we justly estimate the influence of the Hebrew prophets unless we bear in mind the relation in which they stood to the nation as a whole. The truths which they preached stood in striking contrast with the popular religion. They were successively raised up by the Holy Spirit not as representatives of the beliefs and practices of average Hebrew religion, but as champions who never ceased to struggle against the down-grade tendencies, customs, and beliefs of their countrymen. Their preaching could not fail to be unpalatable to the mass of the people, for the simple reason that the God whom the prophets proclaimed was quite other than He was popularly supposed to be. This will become more apparent as we proceed. Meanwhile it is enough to remember that the progress of Israel's religion absolutely depended upon the subversion of false conceptions of Jehovah's character and requirements—a result which could only be achieved by an incessant and arduous struggle on the part of the prophets to introduce a more spiritual doctrine of God.

Different epochs in Hebrew Prophecy.—The Hebrew prophets fall into at least four clearly defined groups.

760-700 B.C.—1. First there are the prophets belonging to the period which preceded the invasion of Judah by Sennacherib's army towards the close of the reign of Hezekiah (702 B.C.); during the last sixty years of the eighth century appeared **Amos** and **Hosea** in the northern kingdom (*circ.* 760-722), and **Isaiah** and **Micah** in the kingdom of Judah (between 740-700).

640-600.—2. During the reign of Manasseh (686-641) the voice of prophecy was suppressed though not altogether silenced. The next great group of prophets belongs to the half century preceding the exile. To this group belongs **Nahum**, the prophet of Nineveh's decline and fall, an event which took place in 607 B.C., and which led to a collision between the two great monarchies of Babylon and Egypt, both of which aimed at acquiring the western territories of the fallen empire. **Zephaniah** was probably the contemporary of **Jeremiah**, whose ministry began about the year 627. To these must be added **Habakkuk**, who apparently wrote during the first years of Jehoiakim's disastrous reign.

592-538.—3. During the exile in Babylon appeared two prophets of great importance. **Ezekiel**, who was one of the captives carried away to Babylon by Nebuchadnezzar in 597, exercised his prophetic ministry between the years 592-570, a period of incalculable importance in the spiritual history of Israel. Towards the close of the seventy years of exile, apparently at a time when Cyrus had already entered on his victorious career and was threatening Babylon, the prophet usually known as 'the second Isaiah' was raised up to be the comforter of his people. The last twenty-seven chapters of Isaiah, or most of them at any rate, may be confidently assigned to the years between 546 and 538. They were most probably written in Babylonia.

520-435.—4. Lastly, there are the post-exilic prophets, **Haggai** and **Zechariah**, the energetic supporters of Zerubbabel in the task of rebuilding the temple. The date of their public ministry can be precisely fixed in the year 520 when the work which had been intermitted for sixteen years was recommenced. At an interval of nearly a century may have appeared **Malachi**, whose period of activity is most reasonably placed between the first and second visit of Nehemiah to Jerusalem, about the year 435.

So far the facts are tolerably certain, and the arrangement of the minor prophets especially is *on the whole* chronological. But there are weighty reasons for supposing that four prophets at least have had a place

ORDER OF THE PROPHETICAL BOOKS

in the collection assigned to them on somewhat different principles.

The book of Joel may be placed where it is because of some internal points of connection with the book of Amos (cp. Joel iii. 16 with Amos i. 2). On similar grounds the book of **Obadiah** finds a place next to that of Amos (cp. Amos ix. 12 with Obad. 19), while the narrative of **Jonah** follows the prophecy of Obadiah, which declares that *an ambassador is sent among the heathen* (Obad. 1). Probably the succession of the books is determined to some extent by an association of ideas or expressions. Certainly Joel, Micah, Jonah, and Nahum seem to have a common interest in the famous passage, Exod. xxxiv. 6 (see Joel ii. 13, Jon. iv. 2, Mic. vii. 18, Nah. i. 3). Nahum and Habakkuk are connected by the title prefixed to each prophecy, the somewhat rare word *Burden* (Massa'), Habakkuk and Zephaniah by the idea of Jehovah's presence (Hab. ii. 20, Zeph. i. 7). Further it is noticeable that a prophet of Israel, generally speaking, alternates with a prophet of Judah. At any rate, Josephus seems to be correct in ascribing to the prophetic writings 'an exact succession' (ἀκριβὴς διαδοχή).

Of the prophetical books enumerated above there are three the date of which will perhaps never be determined with certainty: the books of **Joel**, **Obadiah**, and **Jonah**. It may be stated at once that the available evidence points on the whole to the conclusion that these books, *in their present form*, together with certain fragments now imbedded in the writings of other prophets, are to be regarded as products of post-exilic Judaism, and they may be referred provisionally to the period between Nehemiah and the death of Alexander. There remains one book which is not included among 'the prophets'— the book of **Daniel**. There is a general agreement among modern critics that this book belongs to the period of the Maccabæan struggle (165-164 B.C.); its internal characteristics are widely different from those of prophecy in the strict sense, and the book ought to be regarded as a specimen, perhaps the earliest extant, of an apocalyptic writing. This was a type of literature the appearance of which practically marks the close of Hebrew prophecy.[1]

[1] Prof. G. A. Smith describes the apocalyptic literature of Israel as 'visions of another world that are too evidently the refuges of her despair in this' (*Hist. Geog. of the Holy Land*, p. 35). Some account of the apocalyptic literature is to be found in Drummond's *Jewish Messiah*, and in the new *Dictionary of the Bible* (T. & T. Clark), s. v. 'Apocalyptic literature.' See also the references in Driver, *Introduction to the literature of the Old Testament*, p. 513 (ed. vi.).

CHAPTER II

THE PROPHETS OF THE EIGHTH CENTURY B.C.

Effects of the War with Syria.—Towards the close of the ninth century (*circ.* 815 B.C.), the northern kingdom was harassed by a wearisome and disastrous struggle with the neighbouring kingdom of Syria. In this conflict it suffered severely; the territory east of Jordan, and even some cities on the western side of the river, fell into the hands of the Syrians, and so defenceless was the position of Samaria that her territory lay exposed not only to the invasions of the Syrians, but to the ravages of marauding bands of Moabites (2 Kings x. 32 ff., xiii. 3, 20).[1]

This condition of things, however, was changed on the accession of Joash, the grandson of Jehu and successor of Jehoahaz. We are told that he *recovered the cities* which his father had lost (2 Kings xiii. 25). But the deliverance of Israel was really due, not so much to the prowess or good-fortune of Joash, as to the intervention of the Assyrian power, which had already begun to advance in a westward direction, and now threatened Syria. The power and prestige of Syria was soon diminished, if not altogether broken; and the respite thus gained enabled Israel to recover its strength. In the reign of Jeroboam II., the last king of Jehu's dynasty (781-741), the northern kingdom reached a culminating point of material prosperity. Jeroboam not only recovered the lost territory of Israel on the east of Jordan, but even succeeded in capturing Damascus itself (2 Kings xiv. 25, 28). Israel had now regained the position which it had

[1] On the exposed and weak position of Samaria, see Prof. G. A. Smith's *Historical Geography of the Holy Land*, ch. xvi.

enjoyed for a brief space after the conquests of David. It was the mistress of a territory extending from the Nile to the Euphrates.

Simultaneously the southern kingdom, under Uzziah (777-736), had enjoyed a period of tranquil development, which recalled to men's minds the splendid reign of Solomon. The two kingdoms together had in fact reached the zenith of their fortunes. The standard of comfort and luxury was high; the capital cities of Samaria and Jerusalem were adorned with splendid and substantial buildings; the military strength of both kingdoms was great; riches had accumulated in abundance. The cessation of hostilities with Syria had, in fact, led to a large increase in the wealth and resources of both peoples. Such was the condition of things during the middle period (*circ.* 780-740) of the eighth century.

Moral and social condition of Israel.—But all this material splendour and prosperity had brought grave evils in its train. In the northern kingdom the condition of things was fast verging towards a perilous crisis. While the kingdom of Judah enjoyed some of the advantages which result from a comparatively secluded position, and a relative purity of worship, Samaria lay open to influences which contributed to her decay. 'Samaria,' says Prof. G. A. Smith, 'fair and facile, lavished her favours on foreigners, and was oftener the temptation than the discipline, the betrayer than the guardian, of her own. The surrounding paganism poured into her ample life. . . . From Amos to Isaiah the sins she is charged with are those of a civilisation that has been ripe and is rotten—drunkenness, clumsy art, servile imitation of foreigners, thoughtlessness and cruelty. For these she falls, and her summer beauty is covered by the mud of a great deluge. . . . Poor province, she grew ripe and was ravished before the real summer of her people.'[1] After the Syrian campaign it was evident that the ruin of the kingdom was not far distant.

The simplicity of pastoral and agricultural life had vanished, and had given way before the usual social and

---

[1] Prof. G. A. Smith, *l.c.* Cp. Isa. xxviii. 1 ff.

economic effects of long-continued warfare. The small landholders had been utterly impoverished and were fast sinking into abject distress and even slavery. The rich accumulated large tracts of land in their own hands (Isa. v. 8), while the reckless extravagance of the court and aristocracy exhausted the national resources. On the other hand, the mercantile spirit had received a great impetus from the recent wars. The sins of a growing and insolent middle class began to make their appearance, especially gross dishonesty in trade and harshness in the exaction of debts. The gulf between class and class became daily wider and more menacing, while the social miseries of the time were embittered by the inveterate curse of Oriental life, viz. venality and corruption in the administration of justice. Thus, the oppressed classes were left without hope and without redress.

Condition of religion.—A circumstance which greatly aggravated the social evils of the time was the outwardly flourishing condition of religion. The calf-worship which had been introduced by Jeroboam I., after the separation of the two kingdoms, does not seem indeed to have been an innovation, but it had permanently degraded the character of religious worship in Samaria. Thanks to the exertions of Elijah, during the reign of Ahab, the *cultus* of Baal had been practically suppressed, but the worship of Jehovah under the form of a bull at local sanctuaries like Dan and Bethel, still flourished. Religious worship was at once pleasant and fashionable. There were stated sacrifices to Jehovah, and religious festivals in abundance: the sanctuary of Bethel, where the court was located, was thus thronged from time to time by crowds of worshippers, who regarded the sacred feasts as a legitimate occasion for self-satisfied enjoyment and tumultuous revelry (cp. Amos vi. 1-7, Isa. xxviii. 8). The Hebrew temperament was naturally prone to sensual indulgence, and the excesses committed in the name of religion betrayed the influence of the Canaanitish heathenism which had to a great extent infected the worshippers of Jehovah.

The growth of national prosperity which followed the close of the Syrian wars was popularly regarded as a

comfortable token of Jehovah's favour. There was a
widely-diffused notion that under no circumstances would
Jehovah fail to befriend the people of His special choice.
Israel was the favourite of God, and His interests, it was
confidently assumed, were entirely bound up with those
of His people. Enough, and more than enough, was
being done to secure the divine regard by a richly appointed and well-maintained *cultus*. Consequently any
prophetic utterance which threatened Israel with disaster
was regarded as blasphemy against Jehovah Himself.
Jehovah must necessarily side with Israel against its
foes. To dispute this was to question the very existence
of the covenant-relationship established at the exodus.
Accordingly, a favourite watchword of the time seems to
have been *The Day of Jehovah* (Amos v. 18 ff.), a phrase
which embodied the general expectation of some overwhelming and triumphant display of Jehovah's favour,
manifested for instance in the overthrow of Israel's
enemies. Failing utterly to recognise the essential character and moral requirement of Jehovah, the people
persistently claimed to be special objects of His protection and regard. ' *Jehovah, God of hosts, is with us*, they
declared. Us only does Jehovah know of all the families
of the earth. Jehovah will surely take our part and de-
fend us from invasion or disaster' (Amos v. 14, iii. 2).

Amos, B.C. 760.—Such was the state of things which
prevailed when, about the year 760, **Amos**, a simple herds-
man, from the little town of Tekoa in South Judah,
suddenly appeared at Bethel, proclaiming to the northern
kingdom a message of impending ruin. It may have
been in the midst of some religious festival that the unknown stranger suddenly raised the note of alarm. Amos
was not one of the professional *Nebiim*, at any rate by birth
or training (vii. 14); he was a shepherd and a dresser
of sycamore trees; perhaps he was the owner of a small
farm, or employed on the estate of some wealthy land-
holder. In response to a divine call (vii. 15) he had
journeyed to Bethel, and there, at the chief sanctuary of
the northern kingdom, he uttered his warning (v. 1, 2).
He foretold the downfall of the royal house, the
destruction of the national sanctuaries. and the captivity

of the people. His preaching was received with dismay and indignation, as equally treasonable and blasphemous; for any menace addressed to Jehovah's chosen people was popularly supposed to imply disparagement of the national God. In Amos iii. 2, we have an utterance which must have exactly traversed the general expectation. *You only have I known of all the families of the earth. Therefore* —not, *I will take your part against your enemies*—but, *I will punish you for your iniquities.*

The appearance of Amos may be regarded as a turning-point in the history of Israel's religion. Like St. John the Baptist in a later age, the prophet was sent to be a preacher of repentance. He had been nurtured in the neighbourhood of the wilderness of Judæa, that stern and gloomy region near the Dead Sea, which seemed to bear visible tokens of Jehovah's righteous indignation against sin.[1] To him, as to the Baptist, the word of God came in solitude, *Go prophesy unto my people Israel* (vii. 15). The constraining call was one that he dared not disobey. *The lion hath roared, who will not fear? The Lord Jehovah hath spoken, who can but prophesy?* (iii. 8). And in his book we have the substance, if not the exact form, of the discourses he delivered by word of mouth at Bethel. Its excellence, from a literary point of view, consists in the fact that it 'preserves all the effects of pointed and dramatic delivery, with that breath of lyrical fervour which lends a special charm to the highest Hebrew oratory.'[2]

The book of Amos falls into three well-marked sections :—

(*a*) In the first (i., ii.), the prophet proclaims the judgment of God on the nations surrounding Israel for wilful breaches of the elementary and unwritten laws of natural humanity and good faith. The heathen peoples —Damascus, Gaza, Tyre, Edom, Ammon, and Moab—are judged according to the degree of moral light which each enjoys (cp. Rom. ii. 14, 15). Last of all, Judah and Israel are threatened, as together constituting a single

---

[1] Cp. Prof. G. A. Smith, *op. cit.* p. 315.
[2] Robertson Smith, *The Prophets of Israel* (ed. 1), p. 126.

nation which had been specially favoured, but had hopelessly fallen short of the standard of righteousness divinely revealed to it. The ingratitude of God's chosen people had aggravated its sin, and would provoke a corresponding severity of chastisement (see especially ch. ii. 9 ff.).

(*b*) The second part (iii.-vi.) consists of a series of addresses relating to the sins and imminent punishment of the northern kingdom. It is noteworthy that the crimes denounced are mostly breaches of the moral law contained in Israel's earliest legislation (Exod. xx.-xxiii.): sins against the laws of social righteousness and natural humanity — oppression of the poor, commercial dishonesty, brutish luxury and sensuality, and an idolatrous worship of Jehovah, which ignored both His spiritual nature and His ethical requirements.

(*c*) The third part of the book (vii.-ix. 10) describes a series of five visions of judgment, setting forth the great religious truth of God's government in history. Each vision is followed by a short comment, bringing out more forcibly the lesson which Amos desired to impress upon his hearers. The general teaching of this section is that in His dealings with the different nations of the world, and especially with the chosen people, Jehovah has been guided by the rule of His own righteousness. The judgment upon the *sinful kingdom* (ix. 8) could now no longer be averted: it must have its course. While, however, Amos thus symbolically predicts the coming ruin of the nation as a whole, he makes an earnest appeal to its few righteous members. Their safety shall lie in 'seeking' Jehovah. They are to seek Him in His own appointed way, by righteous dealing and just judgment (v. 6, 14-15). Ch. ix. 11-15 forms a kind of epilogue, drawing a Messianic picture of the restoration of David's house.[1] The ancient promise to David (see 2 Sam. vii. 12 ff.; Pss. lxxxix. and cxxxii.)

---

[1] The passage ix. 8-15 is by many critics regarded as a later addition to the book. See this point discussed in Dr. Driver's *Joel and Amos* (Cambridge Bible for Schools), pp. 119 ff. A similar hopeful epilogue seems to have been added to the book of Zephaniah (iii. 14-20) during or after the exile.

lives in the prophet's memory, and colours his vision of the future.

Teaching of Amos.—What is the chief point of importance in the teaching of Amos? It is his insistence on the necessity of a true conception of Jehovah and His requirements. Jehovah is the God of the universe, because He is a spiritual being whose will for man is the fulfilment of the law of righteousness. The idea that Jehovah was something more than Israel's national God was new to the average Israelite of Amos's day. The ancient Hebrew was not in a strict sense monotheistic. He regarded the gods of the heathen as really existent beings, who in their own territory were scarcely less potent than Jehovah in His. It was only by slow degrees that Israel learned, first, that Jehovah was an incomparably more powerful God than those of Israel's heathen neighbours, and finally that He was the Creator and moral Ruler of the entire universe. Amos proclaims that because God is essentially righteous, He is and must be *the only God*. His kingdom extends wherever the law of righteousness is recognised, however imperfectly, by the human conscience. Judgment falls on the King of Moab who dishonours the bones of his dead foe (ii. 1 ff.), not less surely than on the favoured Israelite, to whom God has vouchsafed a more perfect knowledge of the moral law. Amos's conception of Jehovah has, in short, outgrown nationalistic limitations. Thus he frequently employs the title *Jehovah, God of hosts*—a name which seems to imply God's universal sovereignty, both in nature and in human history. Just as Jehovah creates the stars and marshals their hosts, so He controls the destiny of nations, and rewards or punishes them according to their desert. In a word, He stands in a moral relationship to mankind. Hence fidelity to moral law is the one essential thing in the world, and the will of Jehovah is identical with the law of righteousness. This is what is meant by 'ethical monotheism.' The idea of monotheism was not altogether new; but it was proclaimed by Amos with fresh emphasis, and under circumstances which gave precision and point to a truth that was as yet only dimly apprehended by a few leading spirits among the chosen people. Further, the conception of God as *spiritual, righteous, and therefore one only,* colours Amos's view of history. He, like many of his successors, devotes much space to recapitulations and interpretations of history, past and present. He looks on the world as a moral order, and on national calamities as bringing a message of warning from God (cp. iii. 4 ff. ; iv. 6 ff.). In this he is a true representative of the whole prophetic order, for the prophet is one who thinks of Jehovah as everywhere present and powerful, as the one supreme reality in the universe. Hence his abhorrence of a merely formal worship of Jehovah however elaborate (see v. 18 ff.). Sacrifice without righteousness is no better than the coarsest and most revolting idolatry. It is true that Amos does not expressly condemn the bull-worship of Samaria, though he speaks of it with bitter irony and contempt (ch. iv. 4). At a later time, indeed, Hosea discerns in this unspiritual worship the very root of Israel's ruinous condition. But Amos confines himself to the work of teaching Israel what the religion of Jehovah really demands, and wherein the error of the popular worship consists. He distinguishes between the true religion and the false : between that which Jehovah really demands, and that which is profanely offered to Him in the sanctuaries of Israel. *Seek ye me and ye shall live: but seek not Bethel, nor enter into Gilgal, and cross not over to Beer-sheba: for Gilgal shall surely go into exile, and Bethel shall come to trouble* (v. 4-5). Thus Amos's testimony is an illustration of the fact already noticed that the Hebrew prophets were raised up to be leaders of religion, and that their preaching was necessarily antagonistic to the low and unspiritual beliefs and practices of their contemporaries.[1]

Hosea, circ. 745-735.—Hosea, a younger contemporary of Amos, and a native of northern Palestine, has been rightly described as the prophet of Israel's decline and fall. He probably began to prophesy a few years after the appearance of Amos at Bethel, when the northern

---

[1] On the literary style of Amos, see Dr. Driver's *Joel and Amos,* pp. 115 ff.; Robertson Smith, *The Prophets of Israel,* lect. iii.

kingdom had already fallen into a condition of utter anarchy and misrule (see 2 Kings xv. 14 ff.; xvii. 1 ff.). The first three chapters indeed of Hosea's book seem to belong to the reign of Jeroboam II., since they threaten Israel with deprivation of the blessings which it has so ungratefully misused (see i. 4). The latter portion (iv.-xiv.) corresponds to the wretched condition of the kingdom during the reign of Menahem (745-737), who could only maintain himself on the throne which he had violently usurped, by purchasing the support of Pul or Tiglath-Pileser (2 Kings xv. 19), and practically becoming a vassal of the Assyrian monarch. In less than fifteen years after Menahem's death, the fall of the northern kingdom took place (722). After three years' siege, Samaria was captured by Sargon; the northern Israelites were transported to different districts of Mesopotamia, and their land was occupied by colonists from Babylonia.

The book of Hosea falls naturally into two divisions. In the first of these are related the circumstances which led the prophet to undertake his ministry (i. 2). God's message came to him through the sorrows of his home life. He married a young wife called Gomer, who bare him children, two sons and a daughter. To these the prophet was directed to give symbolic and fateful names, *Jezreel* as a token of the vengeance shortly to descend upon the house of Jehu (i. 4); *Lo-Ruhamah* 'Unpitied,' and *Lo-Ammi* 'Not my people'—names prophetic of Israel's rejection. But Gomer proved to be unworthy of her husband's love. She was unfaithful to him and forsook him. Thereupon the wounded husband, pitying his erring spouse, resolved to bring her back from her degradation. He ransomed her at the price of a slave, and kept her in strict seclusion, in order by a firm but tender discipline to raise her from the depth into which she had fallen, and to re-awaken in her heart the love which she had lost.

In his own domestic sorrow, the prophet was led to recognise a picture of God's dealings with His chosen people. His own experience taught him to interpret Jehovah's love for Israel—Jehovah had taken a degraded and enslaved people, and had betrothed it to Himself. But Israel had only requited the divine love with ingratitude. The pure worship enjoined by Jehovah had become polluted with the depraved rites of Baal-worship; Israel had forgotten the moral conditions of Jehovah's covenant, and had drawn on itself a just and inevitable doom. But chastisement was not the end of God's dealings with His people. Hosea feels himself to be a type of Jehovah, not only in his indignation and grief at Gomer's infidelity, but also in his compassion for her misery. His own bitter experience 'opened to him the secrets of that heart whose tenderness is as infinite as its holiness;'[1] his book reflects the boundless hopefulness of the divine love. Israel will surely learn submission through calamity, she will again yield herself in penitence to God and become what she was called to be, a holy people.

The second part of the book (iv.-xiv.) contains a severe indictment of Israel, and was evidently written at a time when the threatened judgment was now at the very door. We gather from this portion of the book the general features of Israel's condition, the social and moral disorganisation of the kingdom, and especially the corruption of its ruling classes—the priests and princes, who ought to have been true ministers of justice and faithful guardians of the sanctuary and sacred law. Hosea's picture of the priests is very dark. They perverted justice, depraved perhaps by their close association with the court.[2] They were interested in actually increasing the number of sin and trespass offerings (iv. 8). 'Like the sons of Eli, they greedily devoured what the people brought to atone for their sins. . . . Instead of trying to stem the tide of iniquity, they longed for its onward march, with a view to unholy gains.'[3] Hosea even accuses them of highway robbery and deeds of violence (vi. 9). The priests actually led the way in lawlessness and wickedness; their worldliness and carelessness encouraged the people to sin.

In Hosea's view the most serious evil of his day was

---

[1] Robertson Smith, *Prophets of Israel*, p. 178.
[2] Consider the position of the priest Amaziah, Amos vii. 10.
[3] Cheyne on Hosea iv. 8.

THE SINS OF ISRAEL

the idolatrous perversion of Jehovah's worship. As we have seen, it had long been customary to worship the national God at the local sanctuaries under the symbol of a small metal bull. There were three chief centres where a *cultus* of this type was practised—Dan, Bethel, and Gilgal (Amos iv. 4, Hos. iv. 15). The sinfulness of the worship consisted in a breach not of the first, but of the second commandment, and its special danger lay in the fact that the service of Jehovah tended to become 'syncretistic,' *confusing* the God of Israel with the Canaanitish deities who were worshipped in a similar way. The people commonly addressed Jehovah as *Baal* ('owner' or 'lord'), as we learn from Hos. ii. 13 ff. By *the Baalim* Hosea means 'varieties of the one national deity specially worshipped in different localities, such as Baal-Hamon, Baal-Hazor, etc.'[1] It is true that Amos, as we have noticed, does not explicitly *condemn* the bull-worship, but Hosea saw no reason for being tender to it. Nominally the worship of the 'calves,' as the prophet contemptuously calls them, was Jehovah-worship (iv. 15; viii. 13; ix. 4), but in his eyes it was practically idolatry (iii. 1) or nature-worship, inasmuch as it obscured the essential spirituality of Jehovah. The *living God* (i. 10) can have no connection with mere idols. Hence Hosea speaks of the calves as *other gods* (iii. 1; ii. 11, 13). That which Amos had treated with contemptuous scorn, is recognised in its true character by Hosea as a principal cause of Israel's ruin (viii. 6). The 'House of God' (*Bethel*) has become a mere 'House of vanity' (*Beth-Aven*, iv. 15; x. 5, 8; xiii. 2; xiv. 3). Moreover, the sacred feasts were occasions not merely of shameful excess and sensuality, but of ill-timed boasting and frivolous exultation. 'Was it not Jehovah, or rather the *Baalim*, that is, the local manifestations of Jehovah under the form of the golden calves, who had given Israel the good things of peace and plenty (ii. 5)? The whole nation seemed given up to mad riotousness under the prostituted name of religion : *whoredom and wine and must had turned their head* (iv. 11).'[2]

[1] Cheyne on Hosea ii. 13.
[2] Robertson Smith, *op. cit.*, p. 99.

Hosea also, like Isaiah in the southern kingdom, denounces the faithless foreign policy of the rulers (viii. 9-10). There were two factions in the state—one advocating the formation of an alliance with Assyria, the other with Egypt (vii. 11; viii. 9; xii. 1; xiv. 3). This was at once a sin and a blunder. It was sure to lead sooner or later to expatriation (xi. 5), and it implied a sinful distrust of Jehovah, who Himself was Israel's true king. And here we should notice that the idea of a *theocracy* underlies much of Hosea's teaching. In his picture of the Messianic future, Hosea makes only a passing mention of an earthly king;[1] the restored nation is destined no more to rely on horses, chariots, and other material resources. It will live in trustful dependence on Jehovah as Israel's rightful lord and king (i. 7). The book closes with a retrospect summing up the leading features of Israel's sinful past, and predicting its restoration through penitence in the future (xii.-xiv.).

Religious teaching of Hosea.—To this brief sketch of Hosea's prophecy, a few words must be added on his religious teaching, which is very remarkable, considering the age in which he wrote. Hosea is akin to Jeremiah in many of his characteristics. He loved his people with a passionate affection, which taught him to understand in some measure the depth and constancy of Jehovah's love. His favourite word is 'loving-kindness' (*Chesed*), an expression which does not occur in Amos. It describes Jehovah's feeling towards His erring people. It implies that there exists between Jehovah and Israel a relationship of love. Sometimes Hosea describes Israel as the betrothed spouse of Jehovah, sometimes as the child whom He has taught to walk, and tended with watchful care (xi. 1 ff.). Sometimes, on the other hand, he regards Israel as a single person who has entered into a covenant with Jehovah, and taken upon himself the obligations which had been set forth in the *Torah*, or instruction, continuously delivered through the mediation of the priesthood (cp. iv. 6; viii. 1, 12). The word

---

[1] Ch. iii. 5. This, with other passages, is held by several modern critics to be a later addition to the original text. See, however, Driver, *Introduction* (ed. vi.), p. 306.

Chesed is a favourite one with later writers, especially with the Psalmists. As a term of common life (for it is sometimes used of brotherly kindness between man and man), it was calculated to simplify the conception of God. He whom Amos had proclaimed as the righteous judge of nations and of individual men, is regarded by Hosea as the tender and compassionate Father of Israel, as one whose loving-kindness invites the response on man's part not merely of obedience, but of love. Hosea thus anticipates to some extent the supreme truth disclosed in the New Testament: *God is love*. He may claim to be a pioneer in the history of religion in so far as he introduces this deeper conception of the divine nature, which indeed colours his entire retrospect of history. Hence he dwells on the career of Jacob, in whose life chastisement and discipline had been the great factors, but who had ever been the object of Jehovah's pitying and pardoning grace. In Jacob's life the history of Israel was typically summed up. From the days of the patriarchs onwards Israel's development had been controlled by an unfailing purpose of grace, and Hosea bids his countrymen discern in the long story of the past the action of Jehovah's unwearied love. It should be observed, however, that this appeal is addressed only to the few whom the prophet's warnings can move to repentance. The northern kingdom as such had no future; its doom was irreversible. But the penitent are encouraged by the promise of spiritual mercies. The outcome of chastisement is to be Israel's conversion and salvation, in accordance with the inviolable conditions of Jehovah's covenant of grace.

One word as to Hosea's style. The obscurity and difficulty of his book results from the compression and disconnectedness of the thought. St. Jerome says, *Osee commaticus est, et quasi per sententias loquens*. The prophet's style in fact reflects the play of conflicting emotions, and the changing moods of a sensitive heart. A modern writer (Cornill) makes the striking remark that in Hosea's book, 'Like the dreams of a fever-stricken patient, the images and thoughts press and chase away each other.' The style of his preaching must in any case have been very different from that of Amos. If we may judge from his book, Hosea must have been more like a lyric poet than an orator. Each verse of his book, it has been said, is 'like one heavy toll of a funeral knell.'[1]

The fall of Samaria in 722 B.C. marks the epoch in Hebrew history at which prophecy passes from the northern to the southern kingdom. Henceforth the hopes of the faithful were bound up with the fortunes of Judah.

Isaiah, circ. 740-700.—The first of the Judæan prophets is also the greatest, namely **Isaiah**, whose ministry at Jerusalem began, as it would seem, shortly before or after the close of Hosea's career. He received his call in the last year of Uzziah (740), and, during the critical period of Hezekiah's reign, he took a prominent part in the politics of the southern kingdom. Isaiah was apparently a man of aristocratic birth and connections; possibly he was related to the royal family. He was a married man, and two of his sons are mentioned by name. A brief glance at the leading events of the years 740-700 will enable us to form an idea of the conditions under which he exercised his ministry.

Condition of Judah.—During the reigns of Uzziah and Jotham, the relations between the two kingdoms were fairly harmonious; but the attack of Pekah, supported by Rezin of Syria, upon Ahaz in the year 734, induced the king of Judah to look for aid to the Assyrian monarch, Tiglath-Pileser. The position of Ahaz practically became that of an Assyrian vassal (2 Kings xvi. 7 ff.), and thus began that fateful contact between the southern kingdom and the great world-empires of the east which was destined in the future to have such momentous consequences. In Isaiah's teaching the idea of the universality of Jehovah's moral government, previously inculcated by Amos, became through the force of circumstances more dominant and distinct, and indeed the most characteristic feature of the prophet is his unshaken belief in the all-disposing and omnipresent governance of Israel's God. The restless movements of the petty states which bordered on Palestine, and the immense power

[1] Pusey, *Minor Prophets*, Introduction to Hosea.

wielded by the Assyrian monarch, were equally under Jehovah's supreme control. Hence the only course of safety for Judah lay *in quietness and in confidence* (Isaiah xxx. 15), in trustful dependence on the loving guidance of God. There lay before the nation at this crisis of its history two alternatives. It had to choose between passive acceptance of the present political situation, and the futile attempt to hold its own on a stage which was already occupied by great empires with vast resources at their command, and with ambitious aims to carry into effect. During Hezekiah's reign, Judah was constantly tempted to yield to the importunities of Egyptian diplomacy, and to revolt from Assyria, whose iron yoke doubtless pressed very heavily on a kingdom already impoverished by lavish outlay on military defences (2 Chron. xxvi.), and by the recent demands of the Syro-Ephraimitish campaign. In a word, Judah was in danger of yielding to the pressure of circumstances by adopting a worldly policy, and trusting to the material resources on which the great empires of heathendom were accustomed to rely, instead of following the path of simple trust in Jehovah's protection and guidance.

But the spirit of worldliness had not only infected the policy of the southern kingdom : it had entered deeply into the life and habits of society. In the earliest chapters of his book, Isaiah draws a picture of the chief moral evils and religious abuses of his time. Judah was apparently even more subject than the northern kingdom to strange religious superstitions. The cult of the *Ashera* or sacred pole—a Canaanitish emblem of the reproductive powers of nature (Mic. v. 14; Isa. i. 29), seems to have been prevalent at this time. The worship of *Nehushtan* (2 Kings xviii. 4), and even that of *Adonis* (*Tammuz*) was not unknown. The arts of divination, magic, and necromancy were commonly practised (Isa. iii. 3; viii. 19; xxix. 4; Mic. iii. 7, 11). The land was *full of idols* (Isa. ii. 8). It is even probable that some forms of fetichism or totemism, akin to the practices of the nomad tribes of the desert, flourished in secret. On the other hand the social evils of this period were such as usually follow a rapid development of national wealth. Both

Micah and Isaiah allude to the severe sufferings of the small landholders who were ruined by the accumulation of vast estates in the hands of a few, the tyrannical oppression of the poor, and the shameless perversion of justice. The condition of things was naturally aggravated by the calamitous war with Pekah and Rezin, which necessitated the payment of a heavy tribute to Assyria, the burden of taxation, as usual, falling most hardly upon the poorer classes. But what specially aroused the indignation of the prophets was the practical godlessness of their contemporaries, and the fatal blindness of the nation to the divine purposes which were accomplishing themselves openly on the stage of history (Isa. viii. 17). This blindness was sometimes the effect of mere hardness of heart, and sceptical unbelief (Isa. v. 19); sometimes of foolish complacency and shortsighted optimism. The leaders of the nation relied upon their armaments and material wealth to secure them from disaster; but in the eyes of Isaiah this temper of confidence amounted to a practical apostasy or revolt from Jehovah, which could only hasten the day when all the pride of man should be humbled and brought low. The invasion of Pekah and Rezin was in fact the first stage in the fulfilment of the divine purpose of judgment. It was only the earnest of a far more searching and terrible chastisement in the future (Isa. v. 25 ff.).

The prophecies of Isaiah fall into two groups: (1) prophecies relating to the condition of Israel and Judah previous to the fall of the northern kingdom; (2) prophecies concerned with the Assyrian wars. (1) Naturally enough the dominant note of the earlier group is that of judgment. The prophet addresses a perverse and rebellious people, who harden their hearts against his teaching. He predicts the impending overthrow of both kingdoms. In the spirit of the earlier prophets he denounces the pride, cruelty, insolence, and luxury of the ruling and wealthy classes in Judah (see especially ii. 6—iv. 1), while in a later chapter (xxviii.) he foretells the imminent ruin of Samaria. But the prediction of judgment is qualified by the doctrine of a holy remnant destined to survive the impending storm. Jehovah will not fail to bring His righteous purpose to accomplishment. A sifting judgment is to usher in the Messianic age, the blessings of which are to form the counterpart of present calamity. Specially noticeable from this point of view are the prophecies belonging to the reign of Ahaz (735-728). In spite of the urgent warnings of Isaiah (see vii.-ix. 7), Ahaz, under pressure of the Syro-Ephraimitish attack, formed an alliance with Tiglath-Pileser, the result of which was that Judah became thenceforth the helpless vassal of Assyria. It was in these dark days of disorder and misgovernment that Isaiah proclaimed the coming establishment of a righteous and stable kingdom. To this period belongs the prophecy of Immanuel—the child whose very name should be a pledge of Jehovah's protection and help (vii. 14), and possibly also the picture of the Messianic king in ix. 6, 7, and xi. 1-9. It is to the faithful remnant that these promises are addressed: to the little company of disciples who welcome and cherish the prophet's teaching, and on whom the prospect of a brighter future for Judah depended. These are warned to separate themselves from the faithless nation, and to share neither their fears nor their false confidence (viii. 12-18). (2) The second group of prophecies refers mainly to the relations which existed between Judah and Assyria during the period 730-700. During the reign of Hezekiah (728-686) the prophet carried on his ministry under comparatively favourable circumstances. The Assyrian empire was involved in internal troubles shortly after the fall of Samaria, and Palestine enjoyed a brief interval of repose. Hezekiah seems to have resisted, under Isaiah's influence, the temptation to throw off the Assyrian yoke, a course which found powerful advocates among the leading statesmen of Judah. When in the year 711 this party, which favoured a defensive alliance with Egypt, was on the very point of succeeding, Isaiah publicly appeared in the garb of a captive, as a sign of the fate that should presently befall both Egypt and Ethiopia (xx.). The efforts of the prophet succeeded for a while. It was not till 705, the year of Sargon's death, that Hezekiah yielded to the persistency of those who urged an alliance with Egypt. On Sennacherib's accession Merodach-Baladan of Babylon revolted, and Hezekiah followed his example, with the result that he brought his kingdom and capital to the verge of ruin. At first the Assyrian monarch contented himself with ravaging the territory of Judah, and laying upon Hezekiah a heavy tribute; but on second thoughts he apparently determined to destroy Jerusalem, which was strongly fortified, and seemed likely in the future to give him trouble. In 701 he detached a force from his army, which was now engaged in the campaign against Egypt, and sent it to Jerusalem to demand the surrender of the city (2 Kings xviii. 17 ff.). This was the moment of Isaiah's crowning triumph. While the invasion was still imminent he had denounced in stern language the insolent pride and ill-timed confidence of the rulers who said, *We have made a covenant with death, and with hell are we at agreement* (xxviii. 15). He had foretold the siege of *Ariel* (Jerusalem) within a year (xxix. 1 ff.), but with increasing clearness he now predicted the sudden and marvellous deliverance of the capital. Isaiah's confidence in the divine protection, and in the inviolable sanctity of Zion, did not fail him in the very crisis of the peril (xxxvii. 29-35). A sudden and unexplained catastrophe overtook the host of Assyria on the very borders of Egypt. Sennacherib returned to his own land discomfited, and Jerusalem was saved. The faith and confidence of the prophet were triumphantly vindicated.[1]

It is scarcely possible to over-estimate the effect of Isaiah's teaching upon the subsequent development of Israel's religion. It is true that the reformation attempted by Hezekiah—a movement supported no doubt by the prophets—was followed by a disastrous reaction against their teaching in the reign of Manasseh. But the work of Isaiah survived the storm of persecution. For the truths he had taught were cherished by a band

---

[1] Probably the disaster which overtook the Assyrian host was a sudden outbreak of pestilence, which haunted the southern part of the maritime plain. See Prof. G. A. Smith's *Historical Geography of the Holy Land*, pp. 157-159.

ISAIAH'S WRITINGS

of disciples who formed a distinct school of religious thought, trained in prophetic ideas. It seemed to have been from this school that the Book of Deuteronomy emanated—a work which exercised so powerful an effect on the mind of Josiah, and which contained, as it were, the very kernel of the prophetic doctrines. The book, in fact, kept alive at least in the hearts of a devout minority those fundamental religious ideas which had been inherited from the Mosaic age, and had formed the very staple of Isaiah's teaching.

Thus we see the practical importance of the method which Isaiah adopted in order to propagate his characteristic ideas. With him 'the doctrine of the remnant becomes a practical principle; the true Israel within Israel, the holy seed in the fallen stock of the nation, is the object of all his solicitude.'[1]

A few words are necessary respecting (1) the writings; (2) the theology of Isaiah.

The Writings of Isaiah.—1. There are overwhelming reasons for assigning the last twenty-seven chapters of Isaiah's book (xl.-lxvi.) to one or possibly several prophetic writers, the earliest of whom appeared towards the close of the exile in Babylon. On somewhat similar internal grounds, large portions of the first thirty-nine chapters are pronounced to be non-Isaianic: for instance xiii. 2-xiv. 23 (the doom of Babylon), xxiv.-xxvii. (an apocalyptic vision of judgment), the picture of Edom's downfall and of Judah's restoration in xxxiv., xxxv., together with some minor passages (*e.g.* xii. and possibly iv. 2-6). The fact is clear that the book of Isaiah, as we now have it, contains a collection of prophecies which are undoubtedly of different origin and date. When a collection of the writings of the prophets took place, all fragments of prophecy were apparently distributed in different parts of the four books of 'latter prophets' (Isaiah, Jeremiah, Ezekiel, twelve minor prophets). In one of these four books every extant fragment of ancient prophecy had to take its place whether it bore any precise title and date or not. Thus in the very

---

[1] Robertson Smith, *The Prophets of Israel*, p. 209.

process of redaction 'prophecies by other hands would get to be embedded in the text of Isaiah, no longer to be distinguished except by internal evidence.'[1] It is unnecessary to illustrate this point at length. Let it suffice to say that there is little or no question as to those parts of Isaiah's book which relate to the history of his own times; and it is on them that his great reputation rests, and from them that we derive our impression of his supreme genius and prophetic force.

Theology of Isaiah.—2. In Isaiah's theology we may specially notice (*a*) his conception of Jehovah; (*b*) his vision of the Messianic king; (*c*) his doctrine of the remnant.

(*a*) Isaiah is the first Old Testament writer who gives to Jehovah the title *Holy One of Israel*, in order to indicate the relation in which Jehovah stands to His chosen people. All the prophetic visions of impending judgment are based on the fundamental truth that Jehovah is a God of righteousness: His highest requirement of man is well-doing, justice, mercy, and good faith between man and his fellow. To Israel as the chosen people the righteousness of Jehovah had been specially manifested, and by his doctrine of Jehovah's exaltation (cp. ii. 11, 17) Isaiah intends to proclaim the essential supremacy and ultimate triumph of the law of righteousness. This law was outraged not only by the disobedience and apostasy of Israel, but also by the violence and insolent pride of foreign oppressors like the king of Assyria (cp. x. 5, 12, 13). The downfall of the oppressor, no less than the signal chastisement of the chosen nation, involved the exaltation of Jehovah, *i.e.* the manifestation of Israel's Holy One in His necessary hostility to human sin. But as the elect nation, Israel was practically pledged to exhibit a certain moral and spiritual character; a certain separateness from the corruptions and iniquities of the heathen world, marking its special consecration as a 'holy people.' The divine claim which Israel had forgotten or despised, Isaiah continually reasserts. He declares that the holiness of Jehovah must manifest itself

---

[1] Robertson Smith, *The Prophets of Israel*, pp. 212, 213; cp. *Old Testament in Jewish Church*, p. 98 ff.

in judgment; and he warns the sinful nation that Jehovah's presence must needs have a twofold issue: it must bring terror to the godless even while it brings joy to the hearts of the faithful (xxix. 19-24; xxxiii. 14).

(*b*) The prophetic vision of the Messianic king was specially characteristic of the period when Assyria was menacing the kingdom of Judah. The elect nation was threatened in the person of its king, and hence the idea arose of a king of David's line through whose agency Israel should be delivered from the power of Assyria. In the writings of Isaiah, and his contemporary Micah, the predictions of a Davidic king reach their highest point. Isaiah proclaims the purpose of Jehovah to establish a kingdom of peace and righteousness in the hand of a scion of David's house, through whose conquests the might of Israel's oppressor is to be broken *as in the day of Midian* (ix. 4). In vii. 14 the birth of a child in the immediate future is predicted as a sign of Jehovah's redemptive purpose and a token of His presence in the midst of His people; but it is noticeable that *Immanuel* is not said to be connected with the house of David nor is he personally hailed as a deliverer. It is only in ix. 7, 8 that the prince's *Name*, *i.e.* his true character and calling, is proclaimed: and in xi.—'a vision of peace which has ever since haunted the universe'[1]— the character of his rule is described. His kingdom is one of peace, and he is enabled for his high and sacred functions by the spirit of Jehovah Himself. Through him the peace of Paradise is to be restored, and the face of the earth renewed by the true knowledge of God.

(*c*) Isaiah's doctrine of the remnant has been already touched upon. The prophet, with the eye of faith, discerns the true Israel within Israel—an Israel destined to survive the deluge of judgment and emerge cleansed and chastened to be the seed of a renewed and purified nation. This idea of a remnant is indeed common to several prophets. We find it in Amos; it reappears in Zephaniah and Habakkuk; but in Isaiah it forms an integral element of his theology and a keynote of his teaching.

---

[1] Darmesteter, *Les prophètes d'Israël*, p. 63.

Isaiah in fact dissociates the future of religion from the fortunes of the nation as a whole. He saw that the hopes of national regeneration henceforth depended upon the character of a little section of the people, and that the ideal calling of Israel as Jehovah's servant would only be fulfilled through the fidelity of the few. We shall see later how fruitful and powerful this idea became in subsequent times.

Micah, circ. 728-703.—Micah was probably a younger contemporary of Isaiah, but while Isaiah took a prominent and energetic part in affairs of state, and preached to the inhabitants of the capital, Micah was a simple countryman of Moresheth-Gath, a village in the *Shephelah* which lay very close to the scene of the military operations of the Assyrian army. His title *the Morasthite* distinguishes him from his predecessor and namesake Micaiah.[1] Probably Micah's active ministry began at the opening of Hezekiah's reign (cp. Jer. xxvi. 18) some six or seven years before the destruction of Samaria. While Isaiah was a statesman and dealt with matters of public policy, Micah for the most part confined himself to denouncing the moral and social iniquities of his day. There seems to be no good reason for doubting that the two prophets worked in harmony.[2] The reformation of religion undertaken by Hezekiah seems to have been chiefly due to the preaching of Micah, and it is probable that this movement marked the culminating point of his ministry.

An outline of Micah's book will give a clear idea of the state of the southern kingdom at the period when he wrote. It falls into three main sections, each beginning with the word *Hearken*. It is probable, however, that the last section (vi.-vii.) belongs to a later period than the rest of the book, and it is generally supposed by critics to belong to the reign of Manasseh. In the first part (i.-ii.) Micah threatens the kingdom of Judah with the fate now impending over Samaria. He vividly

---

[1] The name means *Who is like Jahveh?* Cp. Ex. xv. 11; Mic. vii. 18. Mic. i. 2 suggests a connection with 1 Kings xxii. 28.

[2] Note their common interest in the passage, Mic. iv. 1 ff., Isa. ii. 2 ff., which is probably from some older prophet.

describes the wave of calamity rolling over the different townships and villages of the *Shephelah*, each familiar name yielding, as it were, 'an omen of calamity.'[1] In chap. ii. the description of judgment is followed by an exposition of its causes, which in the main are offences against fundamental laws of social righteousness. As a member and champion of the yeomanry class, Micah has an indignant sense of their wrongs. He speaks, indeed, of the idolatries of Samaria and Judah, which are doomed to destruction, but his soul is most profoundly moved by the iniquities of the rich. He denounces those who have become possessors of huge estates, formed by dispossessing the poor landowners (ii. 1-2). He rebukes the meaner vices of the trading class, the exactions of petty creditors (ii. 8), the dishonesty of the judges, who connived at the wrong-doing of the rich, and leagued themselves with them in defrauding the poor (cp. iii. 2 ff.). In the second section one point is specially noticeable, namely, Micah's denunciation of false prophets who flatter and caress the rich and powerful (iii. 5 ff.). The sins of the ruling classes, princes and priests, are largely due to the encouragement given to them by false prophets. False prophecy arose in Judah as the result and counterpart of true prophecy, so soon as the *Nebíim* had become a professional order of men, with the failings usually exhibited by such a class. Prophetic warnings of impending judgment were displeasing; it was popular not to believe them (ii. 6; iii. 5, 11). Consequently the false prophets preached an easy doctrine of comfort and security; Jehovah would protect His own; the temple was the guarantee of His favour. The call to repentance was either thought to be no longer necessary, or it was forgotten and ignored.[2] This evil of false prophecy was one that became worse as time went on, and it seems to have reached a climax during the reign of Josiah (see Jer. xxiii. 9). In the days of Hezekiah for the first time we hear of these false prophets (cp. Isa. ix. 15 ff.; xxviii. 7), who encouraged sensuality (Mic. ii. 11), took pay for their prophecies, and lulled men into security, saying, *Peace,*

[1] Kirkpatrick, *The Doctrine of the Prophets*, pp. 208, 209.
[2] Cp. Montefiore, *Hibbert Lectures*, p. 198.

peace, by perverting Isaiah's doctrine of Immanuel, *Jehovah is with us* (Mic. iii. 5-11). The sign of a true prophet, on the contrary, was fearless denunciation of the sins (Mic. iii. 8) which were bringing destruction on Jerusalem; and naturally enough Micah regards the two capitals, Samaria and Jerusalem, as the centres of national corruption (i. 5, vi. 9). Like Isaiah, he discerns in a crushing retribution the only hope of Zion's spiritual regeneration. Israel is doomed to be scattered like a dispersed flock, but the dispersion of the nation is preparatory to a signal display of redemptive grace. Jehovah will once more gather His flock and lead them to their rest, as in the days of old.[1] The humiliation of Zion is to be the divine means of victory over her oppressors (iv. 9-13). She must needs pass through a crisis; she must come forth and dwell in the open field, *i.e.* in a strange land, but there she shall find deliverance: *There the Lord shall redeem thee from the hand of thine enemies* (iv. 10).

Two elements in Micah's picture of the future deserve special attention. First, he thinks of the Messianic age as a time in which the ideal of the theocracy shall be fulfilled. Jehovah shall reign in Zion; the Kingdom of God shall be established under an ideal king of David's line. In this picture Bethlehem-Judah naturally occupies a conspicuous place, for it was the original home of David's family, and the eye of hope eagerly turned thither for encouragement. Micah seems to give utterance to the expectations of the common people in his reference to Bethlehem (v. 2). 'The significance of this prophecy, in its original context, lies in its suggestion of the circumstances under which the Messiah was to be born, rather than in the prediction of the precise place of his birth.'[2]

Secondly, there is a touch of true universalism in Micah's prophecy of the evangelisation of the world through Zion. Zion, purified and renewed by the

---

[1] Micah makes many allusions to the Pentateuch, and describes Israel's restoration in imagery borrowed from the narratives of the Exodus. See (*c.g.*) ii. 13; cp. Exod. xiii. 21.

[2] Kirkpatrick, *op. cit.* p. 217.

indwelling presence of her divine King, is destined to become the spiritual teacher of the nations. And to those who submit to her righteous sway she will be a life-giving power like dew (v. 7, cp. iv. 1 ff); but to those who resist she will be terrible as a lion and destroyer (iv. 12, 13). Jehovah *will execute vengeance in anger and fury upon the nations which hearkened not* (v. 15, R. V.).

It will not be out of place to consider in this connection the teaching of Micah's great contemporary, Isaiah, respecting the heathen, and their relation to the God of Israel. Amos had asserted the sovereignty of Jehovah over the heathen, as their moral ruler and judge. Isaiah goes a step further, and thinks of the nations as offering homage to Israel's God, and recognising His unique power and divinity. Thus, he prophesies that the Ethiopians, in grateful acknowledgment of their deliverance from Assyria, shall bring a present to Jehovah *to the place of the name of Jehovah of hosts, the Mount Zion* (Isa. xviii. 7). And in one celebrated passage the prophet speaks of Israel's two great enemies, Assyria and Egypt, as united to the chosen people in the worship of Jehovah, and thus sharing the blessings of the one true faith. *In that day*, he says, *shall Israel be the third with Egypt and with Assyria, a blessing in the midst of the earth : for that the Lord of hosts hath blessed them, saying, Blessed be Egypt my people, and Assyria the work of my hands, and Israel mine inheritance* (xix. 24, 25).[1] It is hardly wise to lay much stress on the celebrated passage prefixed both to Isaiah ii. and Micah iv., which seems to be either taken from an older prophecy, or composed and inserted in a much later age. In any case, its date is too uncertain to form the basis of an argument; but its teaching harmonises with the Messianic visions of both prophets. The passage represents Zion as the spiritual metropolis of the world, and the nations as journeying thither to learn Jehovah's ways, and to hear His word.

---

[1] Mr. Montefiore accepts the genuineness of this passage, and declares that 'it represents the high-water mark of eighth-century prophecy' (*Hibbert Lectures*, p. 149). There seems to be no convincing reason for doubting that the passage is Isaianic.

It may be thought to embody an idea which was already current in the prophecy of the eighth century.

The third section of Micah's book (vi. and vii., at least to verse 7) is different in tone from the earlier chapters, and seems to presuppose a less hopeful state of things in Judah.[1] The question as to the date of this portion is still unsettled. It is possible that Micah lived to see the disastrous reaction against the prophets which took place under Manasseh; or the passage may be attributed to some unknown prophet of that period. The general character of vi. and vii. is subjective. The prophet speaks of the duty and way of repentance. Thus in vi. 1-7 he describes Jehovah's controversy with His people, and illustrates the contrast between the popular idea of religion and Jehovah's real demand. The prevalent notion was that Jehovah, like the deities of the heathen, required to be propitiated by costly offerings, or even by the sacrifice of human victims (vi. 7), whereas His true requirement had been forgotten: *He hath showed thee, O man, what is good: and what doth the Lord require of thee but to do justly, and to love mercy, and to walk humbly with thy God?* (vi. 8).

The passage vii. 1-7 contains the penitent confession and complaint of the faithful remnant, and gives utterance to a spirit of humble submission to the righteous penalties of national sin. The book ends (7-20) with thoughts of consolation and fervent expressions of unshaken confidence in Jehovah's mercy.

The most striking point in this section is the summary of prophetic religion in vi. 8, which practically forms the substance of Micah's own preaching. It may be compared with the teaching of Deuteronomy (esp. x. 12). It comprehends in brief the final message which the prophets of the eighth century were commissioned to deliver.

There is a remarkable contrast between Isaiah and Micah in one respect. The predictions of the former

---

[1] See Driver, *Introduction*, p. 332 ff., on vii. 7-20, which is thought by some critics to belong to the period of the exile. See the discussion in Kirkpatrick, *op. cit.* pp. 226-230, and Robertson Smith, *Prophets of Israel*, p. 439 ff.

CONCLUSION

culminated in the splendid vision of immediate deliverance from the yoke of Assyria. The Messianic age seemed to be actually dawning. Micah, on the other hand, is mainly occupied with the thought of the inevitable doom about to descend on his impenitent nation; and indeed little more than a century elapsed before the prophet's warnings were fulfilled. Jerusalem was a heap of ruins, the temple desolate, the people in captivity. The solitary hope of a brighter day lay in the undeserved fulfilment by Jehovah of the promises made to Israel's forefathers *in the days of old* (Mic. vii. 20).

CHAPTER III

PROPHECY IN THE SEVENTH CENTURY B.C.

The seventh century B.C.—When in the year 686 Hezekiah died, and his son Manasseh succeeded to the throne of Judah, a violent reaction took place against the teaching of the prophets. It was manifest that the popular religion, at the root of which Hezekiah's reformation struck, was not likely to give way without an obstinate struggle. Few details of this period are forthcoming, but its chief feature was a bloody persecution of the prophets, and perhaps of their adherents : Isaiah is said to have been sawn asunder. At the same time, a revival of the worst features in the old *cultus* took place, and heathen rites were introduced from abroad. Manasseh sanctioned the introduction of star-worship, and the hideous rites of Moloch were openly practised. The king himself set an example to his subjects by causing his eldest son *to pass through the fire* (2 Kings xxi. 6). We are further told that *he practised augury, and used enchantments, and dealt with them that had familiar spirits and with wizards*. This terrible period lasted for nearly sixty years, and the voice of prophecy was practically silenced. It is highly probable however that fragments of prophecy were circulated among the faithful who patiently waited for better days,—fragments the authorship of which it was dangerous to avow, but which were afterwards incorporated in the collected book of 'the prophets.' To the days of Manasseh, as we have already pointed out, may belong the last two chapters of the book of Micah, or at least a considerable portion of them. These, with their lofty teaching as to Jehovah's true requirement of His worshippers, illustrate the effect of persecution in deepening and purifying the religious ideas of the faithful remnant. Before the close however of Manasseh's reign, the voice of prophecy was again uplifted. About 630 took place the terrible inroads of the Scythians, who, issuing from the coasts of the Black Sea, overran Western Asia for a period of more than twenty years, and spread terror and devastation to the very borders of Egypt. Meanwhile Egypt had shaken off the Assyrian yoke, and the empire of Nineveh was rapidly declining before the growing power of Babylon. In 625, Babylon, under Nabopolassar, emerged from a condition of dependence, and in combination with the rising power of Media, laid siege to Nineveh itself, though apparently without immediate success. In 607 however Nineveh succumbed —its fall being sudden and difficult to explain. Tradition says that the overthrow of the city was mainly due to a sudden rise of the river Tigris, which laid a large portion of the outer walls in ruins, thus admitting the forces of the besieging host. Then followed a struggle for supremacy between Babylon and Egypt, a conflict which was ultimately decided by the signal defeat of the Egyptian army at Carchemish in the year 605. The Babylonian monarch thus became the master of Western Asia.

It is important to bear in mind the general character of the period at which prophecy revived. It was a time of unsettlement, disruption, terror, and distress of nations. The incursion of the Scythian hordes does not indeed seem to have actually injured the territory of Judah. The wave of invasion swept, as usual, past Jerusalem, along the coast of the Mediterranean, in the direction of Egypt. But it was probably the terror of the Scythian advance that again roused the spirit of prophecy. Shortly after the accession of Josiah (640) arose four prophets, who are all alike prophets of judgment. Nahum (circ. 626-608) is the prophet of Nineveh's decline and fall. His theme is the impending doom of the oppressing city, which had so long been the scourge, not only of Judah, but of Western Asia as a whole, and which was the very type of insolent violence and godless pride. **Zephaniah** (circ. 625-621) proclaims a universal catastrophe as about to overwhelm the world, and especially the chosen people of Jehovah. *Judgment must begin at the house of God.* The moral iniquities and idolatrous rites which Manasseh had reintroduced were now flourishing in rank luxuriance. Zephaniah and probably **Jeremiah** both discerned in the advancing horde of Scythians, a rod of the divine anger. Hence their repeated and urgent calls to repentance and amendment,— calls which probably did actually produce in the nation a transient inclination to reform. The bulk of Jeremiah's book, however, seems to belong to the period which followed Josiah's religious reformation (621), the effects of which were only superficial; and the premature death in battle of the king (609) crushed any hope which the prophet might entertain of lasting improvement. **Habakkuk**, who probably wrote at the time when Nineveh had already fallen (circ. 607-605), gives utterance to the distress of that righteous remnant which had set itself, in obedience perhaps to Zephaniah's preaching, to *seek Jehovah* (Zeph. ii. 3). He represents the patience of faith waiting upon God amid universal convulsion. Roughly speaking, all these four prophets belong to the last forty years of the seventh century.

Nahum, circ. 626-608.—Nahum, whose name means 'consolation' or 'comforter,' was a native of Elkosh, probably a village in the southern district of Judah, the traces of which have disappeared since the fourth century. His book was apparently composed at a time when the Medes and Babylonians were now threatening Nineveh. There is no valid reason to suppose that the book was written at Nineveh, with which the writer does not really betray any special acquaintance. On the other hand a slight indication that he was not writing in Judah itself is afforded by the fact that 'he seems to regard it ideally as the kingdom of God, rather than actually in its existing condition,'[1] but this circumstance is not of great weight. Nahum ('comfort' or 'comforter') may be aptly compared with the anonymous prophet who nearly

---

[1] Kirkpatrick, *op. cit.* p. 245.

a century later proclaimed a message of consolation to the exiles in Babylon.[1] Nahum in fact idealises *the sinful kingdom* which in comparison with *the bloody city* (iii. 1) might appear relatively innocent. At any rate he shows no consciousness of the guilt and corruption which Zephaniah depicts in such dark colours. His book is rather a cry of agony and revenge wrung from the heart of Judah and the other oppressed peoples who had for so long a time groaned beneath the iron yoke of Assyria.

The prophecy of Nahum naturally recalls to our minds the tradition of Jonah's preaching at Nineveh. If that incident is a historical fact, we must suppose that Nineveh had neglected its day of grace, and had fallen back into the greed and violence (Jon. iii. 8; Nah. ii. 11, 12) of which it had repented at the call of the earlier prophet. Its crying sin was presumptuous defiance of Almighty God. Sennacherib's wars, for instance, had been religious wars. He had blasphemously defied Jehovah himself (Isa. xxxvi. 18-19; xxxvii. 12). Moreover, Nineveh had sinned by her barbarous and inhuman oppression of subject nations, and especially of Jehovah's chosen people. At length the hour of vengeance has arrived. In vain are the preparations made for withstanding a siege. Swiftly and suddenly the blow falls, and Nineveh becomes a desolation and a terror. As a matter of fact the overthrow of the great city was of unexampled completeness. It is possible that ii. 6 alludes to the river Tigris as a principal agent in Nineveh's destruction. In words of touching beauty Nahum describes the consequences for Judah of Nineveh's ruin. Zion is released from the oppressor's yoke— messengers carry the glad tidings across the hill-country of Judæa, and Jerusalem is bidden once more to celebrate her joyous festivals in peace (i. 15).

The style of Nahum is in dignity and force comparable to that of Isaiah himself; it has a vivid and picturesque energy such as only genuine poetic and religious fervour can impart. In his conception of God, Nahum is united to Micah and the author of Jonah by a reminiscence of Exod. xxxiv. 6 (cp. Nah. i. 3; Jon. iv. 2; Mic. vii. 18),

---

[1] Cp. Isa. xl. 1. Nahum i. 15 is quoted by Isa. lii. 7.

—that passage which brings out so clearly the two-fold character of Jehovah—His unfailing truth or righteousness, and His plenteous loving-kindness.

Obs.—The Book of Nahum consists of two odes on the approaching fall of Nineveh (ii., iii.) to which is prefixed a poem of a more general kind, declaring the principles on which Almighty God inflicts His judgments (i. 2-ii. 4). In this poem there are traces of alphabetic structure. The attempt has been made to restore it by more than one recent critic. See G. A. Smith, *Minor Prophets*, vol. ii. p. 81 ff.

Zephaniah, circ. 626-621.—The precise date of Nahum's book cannot be fixed with certainty; but the book of **Zephaniah** seems to supply its necessary counterpart. Nahum, as we have seen, makes only brief passing allusions to Judah. He says nothing of the sins which had provoked the divine judgment. Zephaniah, on the other hand, gives us a picture of the state of Judah shortly after the accession of Josiah, while the baneful influence of Manasseh's reign was still operative. It was Zephaniah's task to proclaim the imminence of the day of the Lord—its nearness and its overwhelming terrors.[1] Like Isaiah, the prophet thinks of that day as an *utter consumption* falling with desolating effect both on nature and on man, and specially on Judah and Jerusalem. Writing probably at a time when the Scythian hordes were threatening the very borders of Judah, Zephaniah represents the judgment as a second deluge. Its range extends from Ethiopia in the far south, to Nineveh in the north. It is swift, searching, and complete (i. 12, 18); even the righteous are scarcely saved. *He shall make even a speedy riddance of all them that dwell in the earth* (i. 18). Zephaniah draws a terrible picture of the religious and moral condition of Jerusalem. The extreme youth of Josiah (he was only eight at his accession) prevented the court from having any decided influence on the habits of the nation at large. The idolatrous rites which Manasseh had introduced flourished unchecked. Idolatrous priests (*chemârim*) were maintained at the public cost; the worship of strange deities was openly

---

[1] *Obs.*—*Dies irae dies illa* (i. 15, Vulg.).

tolerated; the adoration of the sun, moon, and stars was commonly practised. Faith in Jehovah was wellnigh dead. There were many open apostates, and a still larger number who were *settled on their lees* (i. 12), and were atheists at heart, saying, *The Lord will not do good, neither will he do evil*. With this practical apostasy from Jehovah was combined a spirit of moral lawlessness. The very bonds of society were loosened. The sins of the ruling classes especially (i. 8, 9) had made Jerusalem ripe for judgment.

In chap. ii. of his prophecy, Zephaniah presents us with a more hopeful vision of the future. He describes the effect of Jehovah's searching and sifting visitation. He predicts the universal abandonment of idols and the turning to Jehovah of men belonging to other nations (ii. 11; iii. 9). Zephaniah also naturally gives prominence to the Isaianic doctrine of the remnant. In an epilogue which was probably added by a later hand during or after the exile, this remnant of true Israelites, few though they be in number, humbled and chastened by adversity, is yet bidden to *be glad and rejoice with all the heart* (iii. 14). Even in the day of Jehovah's anger they will be hid,[1] and in the Messianic future they will become *a name and a praise among all peoples of the earth* (iii. 20).

Habakkuk, circ. 605.—Habakkuk, who was apparently a Levite (iii. 19), and is distinguished by the title 'the prophet' (i. 1), writes at a time when Babylon was rapidly rising to the foremost place among the nations of the East. His book seems to have been written shortly after the fall of Nineveh, when it was as yet uncertain what would be the issue of the impending struggle between Egypt and Babylon. It is probable that the prophecy belongs to the reign of Jehoiakim, and may be dated shortly before the decisive battle of Carchemish (605). Habakkuk is a representative of those faithful members of the nation who were sorely perplexed at Jehovah's employment of a ferocious, greedy, and lawless power as the instrument of His righteous purposes. It

---

[1] The name *Zephaniah* means 'Jehovah hideth.'

might sometimes seem that after all brute force rather than righteousness was the arbiter of human destiny.

The book is written in a dramatic form: it partly consists of an alternate discourse between Jehovah and the prophet; and if we take into account its leading theme, we may class the book with other products of religious reflection in the Old Testament. The problem which constantly pressed for solution in the disastrous days of Judah's decline and fall was that which Jeremiah raises in his twelfth chapter: *Righteous art thou, O Lord, when I plead with thee: yet let me talk with thee of thy judgments: wherefore doth the way of the wicked prosper? wherefore are all they happy that deal very treacherously?*[1] Habakkuk acknowledges indeed that Judah's chastisement is deserved; but he 'contrasts the guilt of the heathen foe with the relative "righteousness" of Judah, and confidently appeals to God for the chastisement and expulsion of the invader.'[2]

The book falls into three parts. Chap. i. opens with an appealing cry to Jehovah: *How long* is the wicked destined to prosper? In verse 6 the answer is given that a day of retribution is near at hand. The lawlessness and iniquity prevalent in Judah shall be brought to an end: already the Chaldæans are being raised up as instruments of divine judgment. In verse 12 Habakkuk renews his appeal. This time he thinks of Judah's chastisement as inflicted by a brutal and oppressive power which in its turn must surely perish. 'He complaineth that vengeance should be executed by them who are far worse.'[3] Why does the righteous nation suffer so long? why is it meshed in the drag-net of the heathen oppressor?

Obs.—It is fair to say that the above interpretation is open to several serious objections, but in view of the conflict of opinion between critics respecting the structure of ch. i., and the precise references implied in the prophet's complaints, I adhere for the present to what may be called the traditional account of the chapter. For a recent discussion, see G. A. Smith, *Minor Prophets*, vol. ii. p. 115 ff.

---

[1] Cp. Pss. xi. and lxxiii.   [2] Montefiore, *Hibbert Lectures*, p. 206.
[3] Ch. i., A.V. (heading).

Chap. ii. opens with a picture of the prophet waiting silently for some response to his pleading. In verse 4 the answer is given—an oracle which is perhaps to be engraved on a tablet and publicly exhibited in the city (cp. Isa. viii. 1 ; xxx. 8). *Behold, his* (the Chaldæan's) *soul is puffed up; it is not upright in him ; but the just shall live by his faith.* 'For the true Israel, his integrity, his trustworthiness, his constancy, the correspondence of his nature to God's eternal law, constitute a principle of permanence ; he cannot perish, but is destined to live through all the cataclysms and convulsions which are to shake the world.'[1] Then follows a 'taunt song,' pronouncing a five-fold woe for the sins of the Chaldæans : their insatiable extortion, their lust of conquest, their cruelty, their cunning deceitfulness, their idolatry.

Chap. iii. contains a prayer based on the words of ii. 4, *The just shall live by his faith*. This sublime hymn is the utterance of faith, confident and patient in spite of long and wearisome delay. In prophetic vision Habakkuk beholds the advent of Jehovah to judge and redeem His people. He describes it in language coloured by the wonderful deliverances of the past. And when the prophet asks the reason of this great theophany, he receives the answer (13 ff.) that Jehovah is manifesting Himself and marching like a warrior over the earth *for the salvation of His people* ; and that He comes to overthrow the wicked one who stands as an adversary over against Jehovah's anointed one. It is noteworthy that evil is here spoken of as if concentrated in a single personality, *the wicked one*, an expression which seems to include both the Chaldæan and every other God-denying power to the end of time. In the concluding verses (16-19) the prophet declares his unshaken confidence and joy in God.

Obs.—Ch. iii. is by some regarded as a post-exilic composition, of liturgical character, displaying affinities with some of the later psalms. It is headed like a psalm 'A prayer of Habakkuk the prophet' (cp. Pss. xvii., xc., etc.), and has a musical subscription. Hence the question has been raised whether the chapter is pre-exilic, but the point is likely to remain uncertain.

---

[1] Kirkpatrick, *op. cit.* p. 273.

Jeremiah, circ. 626-586.—We must now go back in thought to the thirteenth year of King Josiah (626) when **Jeremiah** first publicly appeared as a prophet. He belonged to a priestly family, and lived at the village of Anathoth, a few miles north of Jerusalem. He began to prophesy in 626 (i. 2), and apparently continued to do so till the close of the year 586, after the capture of Jerusalem. In the early chapters of Jeremiah's book (i.-vi.), we probably find the substance of his preaching at a time when the abuses introduced by Manasseh still flourished. Ch. i. describes the prophet's call. As a preacher of judgment, he is to bear the burden of reproach and isolation: *They shall fight against thee but they shall not prevail against thee, for I am with thee, saith the Lord, to deliver thee.* Chh. ii.-vi. consist of a continuous discourse, describing the idolatry, treachery and ingratitude of Judah, who like a faithless spouse has left her first love, and has *changed* her *glory* in order to follow a multitude of strange gods. Like Hosea, Jeremiah denounces the faithlessness which sought to make alliance with Egypt and Assyria (ii. 18, 36); but appeals and promises alternate with rebukes and remonstrances. Even for the sinful nation a way of penitence and pardon is opened if it will return (iii. 12 ff.). In iv. 3-vi. 20. the inevitable chastisement of Judah's sin is foretold. A pitiless foe is to descend upon her from the north, whose onward march shall spread terror and desolation. The prophet dwells on the moral causes provoking this calamity, especially the treachery and faithlessness of the prophets and the priests; and insists upon the near approach of the danger. We cannot be far wrong in supposing that Jeremiah is here alluding to the fearful invasion of the Scythians already mentioned. But it is possible that the discourse was re-edited at a later time, and was 'accommodated by the prophet to the Chaldæans, who, in the interval, had become Judah's most formidable foe.'[1] It is uncertain however how much of Jeremiah's book belongs to the reign of Josiah. It is manifest that the reformation in the fifth year after

---

[1] Driver, *Introduction*, p. 238.

Jeremiah's call (621) did not produce any lasting amendment; probably chh. vii.-x. (excluding x. 1-16, which is apparently a misplaced section) belong to the beginning of Jehoiakim's reign (circ. 608).

History of Judah, 640-621.—In order however to get a clear idea of Jeremiah's times, we must briefly trace the history of Judah after the death of Manasseh in 641. Manasseh's son Amon was murdered by some of his servants in the second year of his reign (2 Kings xxi. 23). The murderers were put to death, and Amon's son Josiah, a child of eight years, was placed on the throne (639). The government of Judah was practically in the hands of a group of princes and nobles, who are described in the book of Zephaniah as *filling their master's house with violence and deceit* (i. 9), and who connived at all the abuses which Manasseh's reign had introduced. Meanwhile, the adherents of the prophets were biding their time, but it was not till the eighteenth year of Josiah's reign (621) that a brighter day seemed to dawn.

The Book of Deuteronomy.—In this year the law-book was discovered in the temple by the priest Hilkiah. The precise origin and date of the book is as yet uncertain, but it seems to have consisted of the greater portion of the book of **Deuteronomy**, and its date may be approximately fixed by comparing its teaching with that of the eighth-century prophets. Its leading characteristic is that it provides for the purification of Jehovah's worship by centralising the *cultus* at Jerusalem. Its authors were anxious to strike a blow at the chief causes of religious corruption in Judah : the existence of the local sanctuaries, and the possibilities of intercourse with the alien inhabitants of Canaan.[1]

The book was immediately brought to the young king and read aloud in his presence. Josiah was greatly alarmed by the severity of its teaching, and instantly resolved to carry out a drastic reformation of religion based strictly upon the provisions of the newly discovered code. The temple was first thoroughly purged of all idolatrous

---

[1] For a brief but excellent sketch of Deuteronomy, and of the circumstances under which it was compiled, see Prof. Bennett's *Primer of the Bible*, ch. vi.

emblems and usages; the gloomy valley of Topheth, where the terrible rites of Moloch had been carried on, was defiled, together with other sanctuaries which had been dedicated to the worship of foreign deities. Finally a determined effort was made, by the ruthless destruction of the local 'high places,' to restrict all sacrificial worship to the temple at Jerusalem. Thus the objects which the writers of the book had in view were to a great extent fulfilled. The enforcement of the newly-found law-book was a death-blow to the popular worship of centuries. Sacrifice necessarily ceased to be an ordinary incident in the religious life of the Israelite; the practice of it was restricted to the three great religious feasts, when every male Israelite was bound to *appear before Jehovah* (Deut. xvi. 16). It is unnecessary to describe in further detail the effects of the discovery of this book. It was undoubtedly a turning-point in the religious history of Israel. It was a prophetic appeal to the highest and most spiritual ideas still cherished by devout members of the nation. It embodied the moral teaching which was most characteristic of the prophets, and by its publication the foundations of a canon of scripture were laid. Moreover it is important to observe that the book of Deuteronomy furnished the point of view from which the annals of the nation were studied and compiled. The ancient records were carefully collected and edited, with comments and explanations which are written in the spirit of Deuteronomy. Indeed, a regular school of writers seems to have formed itself, imbued with the teaching of the book, and reproducing its special characteristics in their literary work.

Jeremiah's prophetic writings bear plain tokens of the prophet's acquaintance with the book of Deuteronomy. It seems very probable that in his eleventh chapter, where he speaks of *the words of this covenant*, he is alluding to passages in Deuteronomy;[1] and it has even been thought that Jeremiah visited Jerusalem and other centres of population, in order to set forth the teaching contained in the newly-discovered law-book, and to inculcate its

---

[1] See xi. 2, 3, 8, and cp. Deut. xxvii. 26.

observance. But in spite of the effort made by the prophetic party, Josiah's reformation produced no permanent results. It undoubtedly led to a complete removal of the outward emblems of idolatry, but it had little or no effect on the deep-seated moral corruption of the ruling classes. It was arrogantly assumed that Jehovah's favour was sufficiently secured by the purification of His worship. The people, perverting in a one-sided direction Isaiah's teaching, 'pointed to the temple standing in the midst as the *palladium* of their security.'[1] The prophet's stern denunciation of this infatuated confidence and his calls to repentance fell on deaf ears.

The period of Nineveh's decline was one of comparative tranquillity in the history of Judah. In the year 609, the city of Nineveh was again besieged by the Medes, aided apparently by the Babylonians, who had thrown off the Assyrian yoke. It was at this moment, when his inveterate foe seemed to be paralysed, that Necho II., king of Egypt, determined to annex to his dominions a portion of the vast empire which seemed to be on the verge of dissolution. With a strong force he advanced into Palestine, perhaps with the idea of extending the limits of his empire from the Nile to the Euphrates. Josiah determined to resist this advance. At Megiddo, on the plain of Esdraelon, a bloody conflict took place, in which Josiah himself was slain, and his army defeated. By the king's death (609), the last hopes of Judah seemed to be quenched. After a reign of three months, Jehoahaz, the son and successor of Josiah, was put in chains at Riblah, while his brother Eliakim (Jehoiakim), was set up as tributary king of Judah by the Egyptian monarch, who was now 'over-lord' of Judah. The death of Josiah was indeed a fatal blow to the hopes of the prophetic party in Judah. It was followed by a reaction and relapse into the abuses and idolatries of Manasseh's reign. Practically the effect of the disaster on the nation was to divide them into an apostate party which openly abandoned Jehovah, and a band of *soi-disant* patriots, who hoped by means of

---

[1] Driver's *Introduction to the Literature of the Old Testament*, p. 253.

costlier and more frequent sacrifices to win back the lost
favour of Jehovah, and to secure the inviolability of
Jerusalem. Hence the fanatical zeal for the temple and
its sacrifices, which is presupposed in such a passage as
Jer. vii., as if the temple was a visible guarantee of
Jehovah's protection. The prophetic call to moral reformation was forgotten; the manifest signs of coming
judgment were ignored; and Jeremiah found himself
practically alone in his opposition to the religious policy
of the king, and in his unwearied denunciation of the
iniquities and idolatries by which Jehovah's name was
profaned. Accordingly, in his seventh chapter, which
apparently contains the substance of a discourse delivered
in the temple-courts on a feast day, when the sanctuary
was thronged by worshippers from every part of Judah,
the prophet vehemently reproves the vain confidence of
the people who trusted *in lying words* and imagined that
the temple was inviolable. He had already pointed to a
coming time in which men should *say no more, The ark of
the covenant of the Lord: neither shall it come to mind:
neither shall they remember it; neither shall they visit it:
neither shall that be done any more* (iii. 16). He now
predicts the overthrow of the temple itself. The
people had fatally mistaken the true conditions of
security. They trusted in the multitude of their
sacrifices as if these were a compensation for greed
and cruelty, for coarse superstition and faithless unbelief.

It was not long before the warnings of Jeremiah were
fulfilled. In 601 Nebuchadnezzar actually advanced into
Judæa, and Jehoiakim became his vassal. Three years
later, instigated apparently by Necho, the king rebelled
(598). The inevitable troubles which followed this rash
step had scarcely begun before Jehoiakim died (597),
and was succeeded by Jehoiachin, his son. Within
three months Nebuchadnezzar's army appeared before
Jerusalem and laid siege to it. Resistance was hopeless.
Jehoiachin surrendered, and at once a large deportation
of the inhabitants took place. The flower of the nation
was thus carried into exile. The inhabitants who remained
were placed under Jehoiachin's uncle (Mattaniah), a

THE RUIN OF JERUSALEM

young man of twenty-one, whose name was changed to Zedekiah.

After a long time of comparative seclusion, Jeremiah now reappeared as the counsellor of submission to the supremacy of Babylon. Respecting the condition of things in the city, we derive some information not only from Jeremiah but also from Ezekiel, who was probably one of the captives removed in 597. Both prophets speak of the fearful condition of things—the increase of idolatry of a most debased type; the cruelty and injustice of the rulers; the fanatical and misguided patriotism of the populace. Jeremiah gives us an insight into the character and teaching of those false prophets, or false patriots, who proclaimed that Jehovah's anger was satisfied, and that the deliverance of the exiles was imminent. Hananiah (Jer. xxviii.) is mentioned as prominent among these blind guides of his countrymen, and his speedy doom is foretold. It is evident that both Jeremiah and Ezekiel now regarded the exiles in Babylon, who were objects of contempt to the degenerate populace of Jerusalem, as the true Israel of the future. These Jeremiah comforts with gracious promises, even while he counsels present submission to a lot which in individual cases must have seemed undeserved (xxix.). He assures the exiles that in the peace of the land of their captivity, they shall have peace (xxix. 7).

Trusting, as his misguided predecessors had done, to the hope of Egyptian support, Zedekiah broke faith with Babylon and revolted. In rapid succession followed the final siege of Jerusalem and its destruction after eighteen months in 586. The walls of the city were razed; the temple was burned; the king was carried into captivity and his eyes were put out; several thousands of the people were deported. A miserable remnant was left behind; over these Gedaliah was appointed governor, and established himself at Mizpeh.

Throughout this terrible period Jeremiah never wavered, in spite of persecution and wrongful imprisonment, in preaching the duty of submission to the king of Babylon as the one hope of safety. His sufferings must have been severe. He was regarded as a traitor to his country, and on more than one occasion barely escaped with his life. Even after the fall of the city the interval of comparative tranquillity was brief. A band of fanatics, headed by Ishmael, a member of the royal house, treacherously murdered Gedaliah, and the remnant of the people, in spite of Jeremiah's warnings, fled into Egypt. 'There, amid mournful surroundings of obstinate idolatry, his teaching spurned and misunderstood, his country waste and desolate, the curtain falls upon the great prophet's life in darkness and desolation.'[1] According to a Jewish tradition he was stoned to death by his compatriots, yet all his predictions had been literally fulfilled before his death. Jerusalem was a heap of ruins; its inhabitants were settled in the land of exile; the monarchy of Judah, the centre of such high hopes, was extinct; the land lay utterly desolate; as the chronicler says, *She kept sabbath, to fulfil threescore and ten years.*[2]

The Teaching of Jeremiah.—Jeremiah is sometimes compared to Hosea, and the two prophets are certainly alike in their deep religious interest, and in the tenderness of heart which made them specially the messengers of Jehovah's outraged love. Jeremiah is a signal example of those who by the grace of God *out of weakness are made strong*. His sensitive and somewhat timid nature shrank with fear from the burden of his awful commission (i. 4 ff.). He trembled at the thought that he was called to be an exponent of the divine purpose for Israel and for the nations in an age of universal unrest and convulsion (i. 10). But he was destined to prove the sustaining power of divine grace. Alone he was able to face the opposition of the whole land, its kings, its princes, its priests, its people. Again and again a cry of anguish breaks from him as he realises his isolation, and the overwhelming difficulties of his task (ix. 1, xv. 10 ff.). We only know of one faithful adherent of Jeremiah, namely Baruch, with whose assistance he committed his prophetic discourses to writing: both those denunciations of national sin which he had

---

[1] Montefiore, *op. cit.* p. 208.   [2] 2 Chron. xxxvi. 21.

delivered at various times during the first twenty-three years of his ministry, and those words of consolation which foretold the restoration of the exiles (xxx.-xxxiii.). Jeremiah's ministry has been truly described as 'a life-long martyrdom'; his life was constantly in danger from the inhabitants of his own city Anathoth (xi. 18 ff.), and even from his own *familiar friends* (xx. 10). Some have even supposed that the picture of the Man of Sorrows in Isa. liii., was primarily suggested by the afflictions of Jeremiah.

It remains to consider some of the characteristic doctrines of the prophet. Like Hosea, he represents the bond that unites Jehovah to His sinful people as a marriage tie (ii. 2), and sometimes as the relationship of father to son (xxxi. 9). But there is a note of hope in Hosea's book which finds only a faint echo in the earlier prophecies of Jeremiah, and in later portions of his book is altogether silenced. The prophet is commanded not even to intercede for his people: *Pray thou not for this people, neither lift up cry nor prayer for them, neither make intercession to me: for I will not hear thee* (vii. 16; cp. xv. 1; Ezek. xiv. 14).

It was in view of the hopeless outlook that Jeremiah seems to have abandoned the expectation of any general response on the part of the obdurate nation to his appeals and warnings. He could only look to the future, and his gaze was specially fixed, as we have seen, on the exiles who were now bearing the penalty of the national unfaithfulness. From the ashes of the old nation a new should emerge. The issue of the judgment which had descended on Israel, would be the merciful fulfilment of Jehovah's eternal purpose of grace. The true Israel would survive the deluge of calamity, and should experience the everlasting loving-kindness of Jehovah (xxxi. 3, 20, etc.). The worthless kings under whose feeble sway Judah had been hurried to its fall, should be succeeded by a godly king ruling in peace over a regenerate people (xxiii. 5, 6); the ruined city should be rebuilt and *dwell safely*, and bear the name already promised to the Messianic king, *Jehovah Tsidkenu* (xxiii. 6, xxxiii. 16). Most distinctive, however, of

Jeremiah is his prophecy of a New Covenant—a covenant of which grace, not law, should be the special characteristic. The experience of ages had proved the failure of the old covenant to fulfil the purpose for which it was instituted. That covenant was inherently defective. It was powerless to secure the obedience it enjoined; it was burdensome as a law of positive precepts and ordinances; in relation to the removal of sin, it was hopelessly ineffective. Already it was waxing old, and *ready to vanish away* (Heb. viii. 13). Prophecy could only look to the future for a new covenant of grace, under which the heart of Israel should be renewed unto holiness, and the ideal calling of the nation be realised by the free action of Jehovah's love. Under this new covenant, the law of Jehovah should be written in the heart; each soul should have immediate knowledge of God, and the clinging burden of defilement and sin should be removed (xxxi. 33 ff.). It should be an *everlasting covenant* (xxxii. 40 ff.), uniting Jehovah to His people for evermore.

Another trait peculiar to Jeremiah is his deeply spiritual conception of religion. The religion of the future is not only to be without the emblems peculiar to the old worship (the ark, etc., iii. 16). Jeremiah conceives it as involving an immediate relationship between God and the individual soul. *They shall all know me from the least of them unto the greatest of them* (xxxi. 34). The circumcision of the future should be that of the heart (Jer. xxxii. 39; cp. Deut. xxx. 6). True religion should consist in a heart obedient and devoted to Him who *tries the reins and the heart*.[1] And this spiritualisation of religion involved not only the doctrine of personal responsibility (xxxi. 29), but also the possibility of an immediate contact between the Creator and the human soul as such. In this lay hope for the heathen world. There was a natural affinity between the soul of man and God (xvi. 19), and in coming to recognise the God of Israel as the true God, even the heathen would find their

---

[1] Jer. xi. 20; xvii. 10; xx. 12. Some have thought that this expression was first used by Jeremiah.

place in the Messianic kingdom of the future. The grace of Jehovah should not only accomplish the divine purpose concerning Israel, but should welcome into loving fellowship the nations outside the pale of the chosen people (see iii. 17; iv. 2; xvi. 19; xxxiii. 9).

Prophecy thus looked to Jehovah Himself, and to Him alone, for the final accomplishment of His purposes concerning mankind and Israel in particular. In this prophetic expectation of a great display of *grace*, a new epoch in the history of religion begins. The prophets have been justly called 'the spiritual destroyers of old Israel'; for they became the pioneers of a new era when they foretold the establishment on earth of a spiritual kingdom which was to be the true goal of Israel's development; a kingdom no more dependent on accidents of position or on material resources, but on the renewing power of Jehovah's Spirit—a power effectually removing sin, and writing the law on the heart of man.[1]

The short prophecy of **Obadiah** may be mentioned at this point, because of its close connection with a passage in Jeremiah (xlix. 7-22). It seems most probable that both prophets were dependent upon some common original,[2] older than either, which Jeremiah has altered and expanded, while Obadiah seems to have incorporated it with little alteration. We may notice here that verses 10-14 seem to allude to the events of 586, but the book as a whole, in its present form, appears to belong to a later period, when an intense hatred of Edom possessed the restored exiles. This animosity appears in other passages, *e.g.* Lam. iv. 21, Ezek. xxv. 12 ff. and xxxv., Isa. xxxiv., and Mal. i. 1-5. The Jews were never able to forgive the wicked exultation with which the Edomites hailed the downfall of Jerusalem. The book of Obadiah, however, will be considered in a later chapter.

[1] It is impossible here to discuss the complicated and difficult literary problems presented by the book of Jeremiah. The reader is referred to Dr. Driver's *Introduction*, Dr. Cheyne's *Commentary on Jeremiah* (Cambridge Bible for Schools), and the brief sketch in Professor Bennett's *Primer of the Bible*, chap. iii.

[2] The older prophecy probably consists of Obad. 1-9, which, as Dr. Driver remarks, contains no *special* allusion to the events of B.C. 586 (*Introd.* p. 319).

CHAPTER IV

THE PROPHETS OF THE EXILE

THE period of the exile exercised an influence of profound and far-reaching importance on Israel's history. It gave birth to that type of religion which we call Judaism. It transformed a nation into a church. It produced a sharp separation between the mass of the people, destitute of that living faith in Jehovah which might have resisted the disintegrating effects of the surrounding idolatry, and the little band of true Israelites who clung to the teaching of the prophets. In the ruin of Judah, and in the destruction of the temple and city, the prophetic religion had finally triumphed over the ancient and popular type of worship. The semi-heathen conception of Jehovah as a merely national god, who was bound in any case to befriend His chosen people, and who only needed to be propitiated by an elaborate system of sacrifice, had disappeared for ever.

We have a few scattered hints which throw light upon the condition and feelings of the faithful remnant in exile. The later chapters of Isaiah seem to indicate that this remnant had great sufferings to endure and displayed great constancy under them. Their trial was one both of faith and of endurance. The faithful must have felt keenly the tragic irony of events, which had brought an overwhelming disaster, rendered inevitable by national sin, upon a generation which had displayed at least some inclination towards good, and had earnestly set itself to seek Jehovah in His own appointed way. On the other hand, a large mass of the Jews seem to have fallen away during the exile into idolatry. With no living or intelligent faith in Jehovah to sustain them, the lukewarm and worldly-minded practically abandoned their religion, and taunted those who stood firm in their devotion to a lost cause. Thus there grew up through the sifting process of national misfortune, a distinction between the idolatrous members of the nation and the faithful servants or chosen ones of God, who though they were oppressed, despised, and rejected even by their own countrymen, yet clung to the spiritual hopes and promises of which the prophets had been the guardians and witnesses. It is to these that the consolatory discourses of Jeremiah and Ezekiel are addressed. Indeed, during the period of Ezekiel's ministry in Babylon, the sifting process was actually going on. Ezekiel is the prophet of the earlier portion of the exile, and he owed his commanding influence chiefly to his inspired insight into the divinely-ordained purpose and meaning of the calamity which had overtaken the nation.

Ezekiel, circ. 592-570.—Like Jeremiah, whose personal disciple he had probably been, Ezekiel was a priest as well as a prophet. He was apparently a member of the first band of captives who were carried to Babylon in 597. There he settled at Tel Abib, by the river Chebar, where a colony of the exiles seems to have been planted. Five years later, *i.e.* some few years before the final destruction of the temple, Ezekiel entered on his public ministry as a prophet, and the period of his activity probably lasted for rather more than twenty years.

The first part of his book is mainly concerned with the impending ruin of Judah. Among the exiles there were many who fanatically clung to the hope that in some way the chastisement that had descended on the nation would be reversed, or at least its extreme consequences averted. Accordingly, Ezekiel continued to denounce the sins of the people and the rulers, until the fall of Jerusalem confirmed the truth of his warnings.

Ezekiel combined with his prophetic ministry the functions of a preacher and shepherd of souls. He found himself charged with the solemn duty of keeping alive the religious hopes and instincts of his countrymen in the land of their captivity. We must think of the exiled

Jews, not as reduced to the condition of slaves or serfs, but as living in organised settlements and enjoying a fair measure of toleration and even of civil liberty. The want of a temple was supplied by the holding of religious meetings beside the streams of Babylon, where services of prayer were held and acts of ceremonial purification were performed. Probably in course of time fixed forms of worship came into use and houses of prayer were erected, in which the exiles met for the reading of the law and public devotion. Not only in Babylon, but among the Jews of the dispersion generally, these synagogues or *proseuchae* became centres of religious life and spiritual influence.[1] Moreover, it would seem that there was a continuous and regular intercourse between the exiles and those who still remained in Judæa,[2] and just as Jeremiah wrote letters addressed to the captives in Babylonia (Jer. xxix., li. 59), so Ezekiel doubtless addressed many of his prophecies to the inhabitants still remaining in Jerusalem.

Ezekiel then appears to have exercised a regular pastoral ministry among his people; he was a teacher of religion in a somewhat more special sense than the older prophets had been. It is true he resembles Isaiah in his prophetic method—in his visions of the glory of Jehovah, and in his typical or symbolic actions (iv. 1, v. 1, etc.); and he was in a sense the spiritual successor of Jeremiah, whose characteristic teaching he inherits and expands, especially the doctrine of individual responsibility (xviii.). But Ezekiel, in spite of the little we know of his personal history, was clearly a man of marked individuality, who not only comprehended the peculiar spiritual needs of his time, but had the force of will and character to direct a movement destined to be of incalculable importance in the development of Judaism, namely the gradual codification of the priestly law. Ezekiel has even been compared with such masterful personalities as Gregory VII. and Calvin, as one who by sheer energy of character and force of thought impressed an ineffaceable stamp on the religion of his age.

[1] Cp. Ezek. viii. 1, xiv. 1, xx. 1.   [2] Ezek. xi. 2, xvii. 11 ff.

(a) Ezekiel's book falls into three divisions—the first (i.-xxiv.) containing the prophecies intervening between the prophet's call and the destruction of Jerusalem. In these the prophet's work was to dispel the illusions to which many of his countrymen in exile obstinately clung. Like Jeremiah, he sternly denounces the false prophets, who fed the captives with vain hopes, and flattered the remnant in Jerusalem with the suggestion that the tyranny of Chaldæa was already overpast. On the other hand, Ezekiel consoles the exiles in their depression with spiritual promises, not merely of a final restoration to their ancient home, but also of a renewed heart and will, which should enable them to keep the covenant which they had broken (xi. 16 ff.). At the same time, it was his task to deepen the impression made by the more personal religious teaching of Jeremiah: to educate in the faithful a consciousness of personal accountability for sin, and to foretell the advent of a time when consciences should be cleansed and hearts renewed by the gift of Jehovah's Spirit. This teaching was the more necessary in view of the apathy and faithless despair which prevailed among the exiles. They either murmured against God: *The way of the Lord*, they cried, *is unequal*—the sins of their forefathers were being expiated by a blameless generation (xviii. 25; xxxiii. 17); or they sank crushed beneath the sense of their calamities: *Our transgressions and our sins are upon us, and we pine away in them. How then should we live?* (xxxiii. 10). *The fathers have eaten sour grapes, and the children's teeth are set on edge* (xviii. 2). In opposition to this frame of mind Ezekiel insists on the inevitable necessity of Judah's chastisement. He reviews the entire past history of the nation and brings out its essential character, as a long course of ingratitude and transgression, in which Judah has behaved far worse than the heathen, than Samaria, than even Sodom herself (xvi.). But combined with these warnings of judgment, we find that personal appeal to individual souls which is characteristic both of Jeremiah and Ezekiel. Jehovah has *no pleasure in the death of him that dieth* (xviii. 32). The individual soul is of great price in His eyes. Thus Ezekiel exercises a true pastorate of souls. Even his Messianic pictures represent the future prince as a good shepherd, who seeks the lost and gathers the dispersed—in contrast with the shepherds or rulers of Israel who have abused their sacred trust (xxxiv.). Ezekiel in fact regards his own prophetic office in a somewhat new light: the prophet is a watchman, personally responsible for each soul intrusted to his care, and the significance of Ezekiel's conception of his office is that it marks a turning-point in the world-wide extension of Israel's religion. 'A spiritual religion can no longer be a merely national religion; the law that can be written on the single human heart is a law for mankind. On the sense of individual relationship to God a world-religion can be founded, for God is one and His Spirit one.'[1]

(b) The second part of Ezekiel's book consists of a selection of prophecies concerning the nations, especially Tyre and Egypt (xxv.-xxxii.). These form a kind of introduction to the third part, which describes the judgments inflicted on the heathen nations, preparing the way for the restitution of Israel. The general purport of this second group of prophecies is to exalt Jehovah. He who has revealed to Israel His 'Name,' *i.e.* His unchangeable nature, and who has wrought all that He has wrought *for his name's sake*, manifests Himself to the nations. *They shall know that I am the Lord* (xxv. 5, 11, 14; xxviii. 26; xxix. 16, 21; xxx. 19, 26; xxxii. 15). The Name of the Lord shall be made known in the abasing of human pride, and in the chastisement of those heathen nations which have either assailed Jehovah's people, or rejoiced over its calamities (xxv. 3, 8, 12, 15). When the heathen did despite to the chosen people, 'it was not a nationality among other nationalities that they injured, nor a mere tribal god whom they scorned;' 'they were doing despite to the people of Him who was God alone, and were injurious to the one living God.'[1] Moreover, the self-exaltation of a Tyre or an Egypt detracted

---

[1] *Bampton Lectures* (1897), p. 324.
[2] Davidson, *The Book of Ezekiel* (Camb. Bible for Schools), pp. 179, 180.

from the glory of Him who is alone exalted. In presence of the transcendent majesty of Jehovah, the crowning virtue of man is humility. Hence Ezekiel always speaks of himself as a *son of man*, an expression which indicates the weakness and nothingness of human nature in comparison with the Creator.

(*c*) The third part of the book (xxxiii.-xlviii.) contains positive prophecies of Israel's restoration, and the re-constitution of the divine kingdom. It begins with a description of the function of the true prophet (xxxiii.), followed by an ideal sketch of the true ruler or shepherd of God's people (xxxiv.). This is followed by a vivid picture of the spiritual transformation of the land and of its inhabitants by the renewing agency of Jehovah's Spirit (xxxv., xxxvi.). Then follows, first, a picture of the resurrection of the nation from the death of exile, and of its subsequent sanctification through the presence of Jehovah dwelling in the midst of His people (xxxvii.); and secondly, an apocalyptic vision of the invasion of Israel in the latter days by Gog and Magog (xxxviii., xxxix.). The book concludes with a symbolic picture of the condition of the restored people in their own land. This vision of salvation and redemption forms a kind of ideal programme of the future sanctuary and its worship: 'A nobler temple and a purer worship will be called into existence, answering to an ideal which had never yet been realised; Jehovah will return to dwell in the midst of His regenerate people; a life-giving stream will issue from the temple and fertilise the desert; the curse of barrenness will be removed (xl.-xlviii.).'[1]

The main element in Ezekiel's prophecies which exercised a decisive influence on the future was his conception of Israel as *a holy community sanctified by the indwelling presence of Jehovah*. Thus he supplements the teaching of Jeremiah respecting personal religion by the thought of a church or community in which the renewed personality might find an appropriate home and sphere of education. He looks upon the individual Israelite not merely as a soul to be disciplined and trained in the

---

[1] Kirkpatrick, *op. cit.* p. 336.

way of righteousness, but as a possible member of a church—a visible church having definite organisation and clear-cut structure. Ezekiel in fact aimed at securing the remnant in exile against the danger of being simply absorbed in the surrounding heathendom. He recognised the need of definite and peculiar institutions to mark Israel's separate and distinctive character. Thus he insisted on the observance of the Sabbath as a fundamental institution of Judaism, as a sign between Jehovah and His people (Ezek. xx. 12). On each Sabbath day Israel was to realise its unique privileges as a holy people of God, and it was to endeavour to make its daily life correspond with its heavenly calling. The purity of family life especially was to be rigorously guarded, and the duty of loving-kindness towards brethren faithfully practised. In this way the scattered remnant of Israel would be compacted together by the closest ties of brotherhood.

In the vision of the New Jerusalem, which closes his book, we note the influence on the prophet of the teaching of Deuteronomy. The temple is the religious centre of the Holy Land, and worship is the principal act of the nation's corporate life. The ruler (or 'prince' as Ezekiel calls him) has no judicial work in a nation where Jehovah Himself by the gift of a new heart and spirit secures the perfect observance of His law, and by miraculous intervention wards off the assaults of heathen foes. The prince is simply a representative of the nation in its religious capacity; his chief function is to care for the temple and to defray the cost of the sacrificial worship by receiving the religious offerings of the people.

In these chapters we find the first sketch of an ideal theocracy—the state having been transformed, so to speak, into a congregation or church. The idea that underlies the entire sketch is, as we have seen, that of a community sanctified by the indwelling presence of Jehovah: *The name of the city from that day shall be, Jehovah is there* (xlviii. 35). The Messianic picture of Ezekiel's earlier chapters melts into a vision characteristic of the priestly class to which the prophet belonged: the vision of Jehovah's enthronement and permanent presence in the midst of His people.

We have noticed that Ezekiel may be regarded on the one hand as a preacher of penitence and a pastor of souls; on the other, as a prophet whose function it was to mould the thought and direct the aims of the future. As a preacher his task was to inculcate true ideas of God: 'to create a true religious hopefulness in the mercy of God, and a true religious humility as to the merits of man'[1] 'Humility combined with hope,'—this was his message to the exiles. The duty of humility was in fact based upon the self-revelation of God, and a large part of Ezekiel's work may be correctly described as 'theodicy,' *i.e.* the endeavour to justify to man the dealings of Jehovah with His people. The vindication of the divine Majesty demanded on the one hand the chastisement of an idolatrous and rebellious people; on the other hand, it must be guarded from such profanation in the eyes of the heathen as would be involved in Israel's utter destruction. In this transcendent idea of Jehovah's glory, and of the honour of His Name, is rooted Ezekiel's view of the past and his hope for the future. His conception of the nation's previous history is dark and pessimistic, and it closely resembles the view which evidently dominated the compilers and editors of the historical books. Israel's past career has been a long story of apostasy and rebellion on the nation's part, and of long-suffering tenderness on the part of Jehovah. But in the age-long loving-kindness of God, Ezekiel finds hope for the future. He believes that Israel will rise to the fulfilment of its ideal calling, not through any effort or repentance of its own, but as the result of Jehovah's grace. Jehovah will bestow upon His people *a new heart, and put a new spirit within them,* thus enabling them to keep His covenant and to execute His will (xxxvi. 26). The promise of divine grace is also a call to individual self-humiliation. As we have seen, the exiles were oppressed with the moral difficulty involved in their present forlorn condition. How was it that judgment had descended indiscriminately on the good and on the evil,—on those who faithfully served

---

[1] Montefiore, *op. cit.* p. 245.

Jehovah and those who regarded Him not? Surely the fathers had *eaten sour grapes, and the children's teeth were set on edge.* Ezekiel does not attempt directly to meet this difficulty. He confines himself to delivering God's present message: *the soul that sinneth it shall die. The son shall not bear the iniquity of the father, neither shall the father bear the iniquity of the son* (xviii. 20). The doctrine of individual responsibility is stated without qualification, and in a way that raises further inevitable questionings; but the teaching of Ezekiel at least prepares the way for a more satisfying theory as to the relation of the individual to God. Thus the book of Ezekiel practically ends with a message of hope. The exiles who are crushed by the overwhelming burden of their sins, who pine away in their iniquities, are bidden not to despair. They have but to *cast away* their *transgressions, to turn* themselves *and live* (xviii. 31, 32). The prophet, in fact, proclaims the gospel of God's unchangeable goodwill towards man, His call to true repentance, and His free offer of cleansing and renewing grace. On the other hand, as a prophet Ezekiel may be fairly described as one of the founders of Judaism, for the ideas, which he inherits from the older prophecy, are set in a framework of legalism. But the prophet is chiefly concerned with the re-constitution of the nation on a basis corresponding to its ideal vocation. The sketch of a new sanctuary and worship doubtless exercised a powerful influence on the priestly legislation of the Pentateuch. It set before Israel a new hope—a hope which answered to the needs of a nation with none but a religious future before it. And it must be remembered that there underlies the vision of the restored temple a spiritual idea, that of Jehovah's everlasting presence with His people, and further that a great moral change in the people is pre-supposed. The nation in the midst of which Jehovah sets up His sanctuary for evermore is a nation already prepared for His indwelling presence by an entire regeneration of heart and life. In spite of its legalistic framework, Ezekiel's vision of the New Jerusalem is the product of lofty spiritual hopes.

Literary activity during the Exile.—Ezekiel's ministry apparently ceased about the year 570, and the period which followed seems to have been comparatively uneventful. It is most probable however that there was much literary activity among the Jews at this time. The historical annals of Israel's past were collected and gradually compiled in a permanent shape. Israel was, as it were, making an inventory of its spiritual possessions.[1] The historical books are in fact specimens of 'applied prophecy.' The editors and compilers make it their aim to explain Israel's present forlorn condition by reference to its past career. Hence the history is from one point of view essentially a theodicy. The calamities of Israel are uniformly regarded by the compilers as the necessary chastisement of national sin, especially of idolatry. The sins of Jeroboam and of Manasseh had brought upon Israel an inevitable retribution which the short-lived repentance of the nation under Josiah was powerless to avert. But the pessimistic survey of the past was qualified by hopes of a brighter future, as the seventy years of exile predicted by Jeremiah began to draw towards their close. Indeed, with the death in 561 of Nebuchadnezzar, its greatest monarch and virtual second founder, the Babylonian empire began to fall into decay. In 550 Cyrus of Persia made himself master of Media. In 547 Nabonnedos, a pious, peaceful, and learned monarch, entered into a defensive alliance with Egypt, Lydia, and Sparta, against the growing power of Cyrus. Almost without effort Cyrus became master of Babylon in 538, and the hour of Israel's redemption from captivity had arrived.

The second Isaiah, circ. 550.—It was apparently in the period of Cyrus's earlier victories that the voice of prophecy was again raised by one of its most glorious representatives—the unknown prophet to whom the last twenty-seven chapters of Isaiah's book are usually ascribed. It has been questioned by some modern critics whether these twenty-seven chapters all proceed from one author, but there is little doubt that about nineteen

---

[1] See Additional Note A, p. 76.

of the twenty-seven may be reasonably ascribed to this great unknown comforter of exiled Israel.[1] For the characteristic message of the prophet is contained in his opening words, *Comfort ye, comfort ye, my people, saith your God. Speak ye comfortably to Jerusalem* (xl. 1). He seems to take up that *word of consolation* with which former prophets had usually closed their predictions of judgment. 'God's righteousness which erewhile could only be made manifest in judgment, must now be expressed in salvation.'[2] For Israel's deliverance was not merely the restoration of a despised and down-trodden people to its own land; it was a decisive revelation of the character of Jehovah, and of those gracious purposes for the heathen of which Israel was called to be the instrument and minister. Hence the prophet combines with his message much theological teaching of which the main points are the following:—

(*a*) First, he proclaims the omnipotence of Jehovah. No human power can hinder His work, or arrest the fulfilment of His promises. Jehovah is the only God in heaven and earth, the sole ruler of the universe, the sole disposer of the fates of nations. In the second Isaiah the conception of *God Himself* as executing His own eternal purpose of grace, practically supersedes the vision of a Davidic Messiah, destined to be the divinely directed and triumphant deliverer of Israel. *The Lord God will come with strong hand, and his arm shall rule for him* (xl. 10). Like a shepherd He will lead His scattered flock homeward to their ancient fold.

The omnipotence of Jehovah—this then is the mastertruth proclaimed by the prophet. Hence the scorn which he lavishes upon the idols of the heathen, those helpless blocks of wood and stone to which vain man presumptuously likens God (xl. 18). The prophet can scarcely find words adequate to express his contempt. In comparison of the only God the idols are *less than nothing and vanity* (xl. 17). Jehovah alone is a *personal* being, having will, character, foresight, power. He alone can foretell the future (xliii. 9-13, etc.) The prophet's

---

[1] See Additional Note B, p. 77.   [2] Montefiore, *op. cit.* p. 265.

derisive challenge to produce instances in which the heathen gods have predicted future events, meets with no response. Jehovah alone is the God of prophecy, the God who has long since foretold Israel's redemption from captivity, and whose predictions, uttered by the mouth of His messengers, have been already repeatedly accomplished. Indeed, the teaching of the prophet on this theme amounts to a sustained polemic, the more impassioned perhaps because in Babylon idolatry was practised on such an imposing scale, and must have produced on the exiled Jews so overwhelming an impression.

(b) Secondly, the originality of the second Isaiah is most clearly seen, in his indication of the instrument through whom Israel's deliverance is to be accomplished. No prince of Hebrew descent, no scion of David's house, is to be the restorer of Israel, but the Persian monarch whose rapid series of conquests was already, no doubt, enkindling the hopes of the exiles. *I have raised up one from the north, and he shall come: from the rising of the sun shall he call upon my name: and he shall come upon princes as upon mortar and as the potter treadeth clay* (xli. 25). Cyrus is hailed as the *shepherd* of Jehovah, who *shall perform all* His *pleasure* (xliv. 28); as the *anointed* of Jehovah, before whom the strength of kings shall melt away, and the gates of brass and iron be broken in pieces (xlv. 1 ff.). But Jehovah's employment of Cyrus as His instrument is after all only an additional proof of that supreme sovereignty and power of initiative in the possession of which Jehovah is unique. The doctrine of Isaiah, that the moral government of Jehovah embraces the entire history of the world and that His purpose of grace accordingly extends to all nations, is expanded by the prophet of the exile into the doctrine that since Jehovah is the one God of the universe, Israel is His prophet and chosen servant charged with a mission to the heathen. For the sake of this elect servant the whole course of history is providentially guided and controlled, but the redemptive purpose of God embraces humanity at large. The goal of the world-movement is a catholic Church: *Mine house shall be called an house of prayer for all peoples* (lvi. 7).

(c) Thirdly, to the newly-realised function of Israel corresponds a title, which sets forth at once the truth of the nation's election, and the purpose which that election was designed to fulfil. Israel is *the servant of Jehovah*. The title which had belonged to individuals like Moses, Joshua, and David, is now transferred to the nation itself viewed in its corporate capacity. To this 'servant' the consolations and promises of Deutero-Isaiah are addressed (xli. 8-16). The servant is reminded of his splendid vocation—to be *a light of the Gentiles, to open the blind eyes, to bring out prisoners from the dungeon, and them that sit in darkness out of the prison-house* (xlii. 5-7). The sufferings which the nation had undergone were divinely intended to prepare it for the fulfilment of its mission. But hitherto the chastisement has borne fruit only in humiliation and distress. The actual Israel of the exile has utterly failed; it has been brought low for its sins. It is blind, deaf, and ensnared (xlii. 18 ff.), but nevertheless its ideal character remains indelible. The very unworthiness and weakness of Jehovah's chosen instrument serves to make it the more submissive to the divine leading. Through its very sufferings, Israel is destined to bring blessing to the world, and so to accomplish the ancient promise concerning Abraham and his seed.

There is, however, another division of the book in which *the servant of Jehovah* seems to be expressly distinguished from the nation: the ultimate purpose of Jehovah, both for Israel and for the heathen, is to find accomplishment through the agency of one whom the nation at large despises and rejects. In xlix.-liii. the servant speaks as one conscious of a mission, both to his own people and to the Gentiles (xlix. 3 ff.). Thus, whereas in the first nine chapters the whole nation is addressed as Jehovah's servant, the forty-ninth and following chapters speak of an individual person who seems to represent the ideal Israel, and successfully accomplishes the work which the actual Israel had failed to achieve.

This work is conceived, speaking broadly, as that of a divinely commissioned *prophet*, through whose agency and teaching Israel is to be restored to its former estate, and the Gentile world is to be brought to a knowledge of the true religion (xlii. 1-6, xlix. 5-8). At the hands of his own people the prophet is to meet with contumely and contempt (l. 4-9). He is even to suffer vicariously for the sins of others, to be despised, rejected, and slain (liii.), but only in order that through death he may rise to a new and glorified life of fruitfulness and power, in which *he shall see of the travail of his soul, and shall be satisfied* (liii. 11, 12). On a general review of all the passages bearing upon the work and mission of the servant, the safest and most satisfactory conclusion seems to be that of Delitzsch and others. 'The idea of the servant of Jehovah, assumed, as it were, the form of a pyramid, the base was the people of Israel as a whole, the central section was Israel according to the Spirit, and the apex is the person of the mediator of salvation springing out of Israel. And the last of the three is regarded (1) as the centre of the circle of the promised kingdom—the *second David*; (2) the centre of the circle of the people of salvation—the *second Israel*; (3) the centre of the circle of the human race—the *second Adam*.'[1]

This great conception of Jehovah's servant arose as the result of the circumstances in which Israel was now placed. Its fortunes were no longer bound up with those of the monarchy, for the royal house was well-nigh extinguished, and the throne of David cast down. Thus the figure of the king, which is so conspicuous in the prophecies of Isaiah, finds no place in the pages of the exilic prophet. His hopes are rather fixed upon the suffering people of God, that faithful remnant which, through calamity, had come to realise the real significance of Israel's election, and the true tendency and drift of its entire history.

One slight but clear indication of the later Isaiah's date appears in his vision of the future, which is coloured by the hopes and ideals of Judaism. Jeremiah, like the writer of Deuteronomy, had spoken of a circumcision of the heart, and of a spiritual worship without temple or ark; but the second Isaiah conceives the holiness of the renewed Jerusalem somewhat as Ezekiel does, that is, as consisting in a perfect observance of the ceremonial law, and in the

[1] Delitzsch on Isaiah xlii. 1.

exaltation of Zion as the metropolis of nations. 'The Gentiles are regarded mainly from the point of view of increasing the wealth and glory of Israel by the services and tribute which they willingly pay to it' [1] (lx.-lxii.). As in the case of Ezekiel however the idea underlying the vision of a restored worship and ceremonial is a purely spiritual one. The renewed glory of Jerusalem and of the temple arises from the fact that Jerusalem is the fountain of religious truth to the universe. 'Jerusalem is the world's capital because Jehovah dwells there.' [2]

The return from Exile, 537 B.C.—The liberation of the exiles probably followed within a few years after the last prophecies of the second Isaiah were uttered. With lightning-like rapidity Cyrus advanced and delivered his final blow. In the year 538 he entered Babylon, and though from motives of policy as it seems he did not fulfil the prophet's hopes by putting an end to the idolatry of the great city, he gave permission both to the Jews and to exiles belonging to other nations to return to their own land. In 537, a start was made, and though a comparatively small company (42,360) availed themselves of Cyrus's permission, they were probably so selected as to be representative of the whole nation, and certainly the spiritual hopes of the Jewish people were bound up with their fortunes.

Additional Note A

Literary activity during the Exile

For an admirable account of the gradual compilation of the historical books, see Professor Bennett's *Primer of the Bible*, part i., ch. vi.

Two schools of writers were successively at work during the exile: first, the 'Deuteronomic editors' who gathered together into a connected historical work the annals and other ancient documents relating to the earlier history of Israel. The result of their labours was 'the combination of the double Prophetic document (JE) with an expanded edition of Josiah's law-book, and works which were substantially our Judges, Samuel, and Kings. The

---

[1] Montefiore, *op. cit.* p. 281.   [2] *Ibid.* p. 282.

editing was done at different times and by different hands; but the editors were alike devoted to the faith formulated in Deuteronomy, and their work must have had continuity and concert.'

The second school of writers was sacerdotal. It devoted itself to the task first of codifying the ancient ' Law of Holiness' (Lev. xvii.-xxvi., etc.), and perhaps at a later time of compiling the so-called 'priestly code' (P). This was not a new code of law, but rather a kind of exposition of all the ancient customs and usages connected with the Levitical priesthood, the national sanctuary and its worship. ' It consisted of a collection of laws set in a historical framework, furnished with a brief system of genealogies and chronology which extends in unbroken continuity from beginning to end.'[1] The priestly code was probably combined with the Deuteronomic work above mentioned at the close of the exile, and thus the ' Pentateuch ' in its present form was probably completed before Ezra visited Jerusalem in 458.

Additional Note B

The Authorship of Isaiah xl.-lxvi.

In the foregoing pages the above chapters of the book of Isaiah have been treated as forming a literary whole, but a careful examination of the book has led critics to distinguish between its different sections. The 'servant passages' for instance are regarded as the work of one author (xlii. 1-4 ; xlix. 1-6 ; l. 4-9 ; lii. 13-liii. 12); while certain chapters, *e.g.* lvi. 9-lvii. 21, lviii.-lix., seem to presuppose a situation quite other than that of the captivity. Again lx.-lxii., and lxiii.-lxvi., appear to presuppose the circumstances of a period long subsequent to the restoration. The whole question is very difficult and complicated, and for the present any expression of opinion by a non-expert would be premature. The reader is referred to Dr. Driver's *Introduction,* to a series of papers by Dr. Davidson in the *Expositor* for 1883, 1884, and to Dr. Cheyne's well-known works.

[1] Bennett, *op. cit.* ch. viii. ; cp. Montefiore, *Hibbert Lectures,* No. vi.

CHAPTER V

AFTER THE EXILE

The return of the Exiles.—With the return from Babylon a new epoch in Israel's history opens. The first care of the restored exiles was to repair the ruined altar of burnt-offering, and to reorganise the sacrificial worship; but the foundation of the temple had scarcely been laid before the opposition of the Samaritans[1] brought the work to a standstill (Ezra iii., iv.). For about sixteen years this unhappy state of things continued, until in 520 the voice of prophecy was again uplifted. The period was one of severe distress in Judæa, and of political excitement in the East. Judæa was suffering from prolonged famine and scarcity; and Darius had recently raised himself to the throne of Persia after its brief usurpation by a Magian adventurer (521). The temple was left unfinished, but the progress of the work was hindered even more by the apathy of the exiles than by the hostility of the Samaritans.

Haggai, 520 B.C.—It was at this critical moment that the venerable prophet **Haggai**, who had apparently seen with his own eyes the city and temple before its destruction in 586, appeared to warn his countrymen that the present distress was a divine chastisement for the supineness which had left the temple for nearly seventeen years in ruins. *Is it time*, he asked, *for ye yourselves to dwell in your ceiled houses, and this house lie waste? Now therefore thus saith the Lord of hosts, Consider your ways* (Hag. i. 4, 5). It seems

---

[1] This term is not strictly accurate; it includes the descendants of the ten tribes, as well as the alien settlers who had been transplanted from Assyria (2 Kings xvii. 24).

indeed that the Jews had been too easily daunted by the opposition of their adversaries. They said to themselves that the time was not come for Jehovah's house to be built (Hag. i. 2). They may have supposed that the period of seventy years since the destruction of the temple was not yet completed. In any case there seems to have been a widespread feeling of depression among the exiles. They had returned cheered and uplifted by the glowing oracles of the great prophet of the exile (see Isa. li. 11; lii. 7 ff.; lv. 12), but their hopes were speedily quenched. Jehovah's promises seemed to have failed; all went on as before. Instead of Babylon, another heathen power, Persia, was Israel's over-lord. Jerusalem was a wretched and comfortless town without walls, inhabited by a poverty-stricken population. It was indeed only the shadow of its former self. It was no wonder that tears and lamentations mingled with the thanksgivings with which the foundations of the temple were laid in 536 (Ezra iii. 12, 13; cp. Hag. ii. 3).

But nevertheless Haggai was right in his conception of the gravity of this crisis in Israel's history. The Jews were contentedly leaving the temple in ruins; but, humanly speaking, a visible and central sanctuary was vitally necessary for the maintenance of Israel's faith. 'The temple was the outward symbol of the dwelling of God in the midst of Israel. To let it be neglected was, alike for themselves, and in the sight of the nations around, a practical denial of the truth which gave meaning to their return from exile. . . . The temple was the necessary centre for the people, whose bond of unity must henceforth be their religion.'[1] For the needs of the period of 500 years which was yet to elapse before the coming of Christ, the existence of a national sanctuary was in fact indispensable. Two persons were specially prominent among the 'children of the captivity': Zerubbabel, who as the heir of Jehoiachin was the official representative of David's house, and who was probably appointed governor of Judah by Cyrus;[2] and Joshua the priest, the

---

[1] Kirkpatrick, *op. cit.* p. 427.
[2] Some critics, *e.g.* Cornill, suppose that a Persian commissary called Sheshbazzar was the nominal governor of Judah, and that

grandson of Seraiah, who had been put to death by Nebuchadnezzar. Accordingly these two names figure in the prophecy of this period, but after its brief revival in the person of Zerubbabel, the house of David sank into complete obscurity, and the leadership of the nation was practically left in the hands of the priesthood. It is specially to Zerubbabel and Joshua that Haggai's exhortation is addressed, bidding them be strong and work, and foretelling the future glory of the temple. Chap. ii. 1-9 contains a message of encouragement and consolation for those who had resumed the building of the temple, and were distressed by its poverty and insignificance. The revival of Messianic hopes appears in the special message to Zerubbabel as the *servant of Jehovah* (ii. 23). In the impending overthrow of thrones and kingdoms, Zerubbabel, as the representative of his people, is to be the *signet, i.e.* the most treasured possession of Jehovah. Thus the doom pronounced on Jeconiah is reversed (Jer. xxii. 24).

Three separate prophecies of Haggai seem to have been delivered in the 6th, 7th, and 9th months of the year 520. His voice was not yet silent before Zechariah appeared to support the older prophet. His first prophecy was probably delivered in the 8th month of the same year, 520. The general subject of Zechariah's preaching, as we gather from the part (i.-viii.) that sound criticism warrants us in ascribing to him, is the same as that of Haggai, viz. the restoration of the temple, and the revival of Messianic royalty in the person of Zerubbabel.

Zechariah was still only a youth when he was called to the prophetic office (ii. 4). Probably he was of priestly descent, and may have been himself a priest (Neh. xii. 16). His book reflects to some extent the spirit of anxious and even painful interest with which the Jews were then watching the course of events in the great empires surrounding them. The least dis-

Zerubbabel, as one of the council of twelve elders, actually administered the affairs of the province. But it is quite possible that Sheshbazzar is a Persian title of Zerubbabel. See Ryle, *Ezra and Nehemiah,* xxxi. ff.

turbance was apt to be taken as a sign that Israel's period of humiliation was at an end, and that her exaltation was about to begin. The series of visions in i.-vi. of Zechariah's book describes with progressive clearness the destiny and fortunes of God's people, and is intended to encourage the people and its leaders. Incidentally we learn how close and strong were the links of connection between the Jews who remained in Babylon and the 'children of the captivity' (vi. 15). The crowning of Joshua may have been a typical expression of the fact that the Jews dispersed abroad still shared the hopes of Israel, and still looked for the coming of the priest-king who should be Jehovah's representative, and the sharer of His throne (vi. 9-15).[1] With the coming of the Messianic priest is connected the building of the temple, and the removal of sin (vi. 12 ff.).

The eight visions of Zechariah are symbolic of Israel's future fortunes. The first vision of four horsemen on divers-coloured horses (i. 7-17) represents the instruments of the divine vengeance prepared to execute judgment on the whole earth. It implies the nearness of Zion's restoration (cp. Rev. vi. 1-10). The horns of iron (i. 18-21) are emblems of the world-power which has scattered Israel. Beside them are four smiths ready to shatter them. The vision of the man with a measuring line (ii.) speaks of protection. Jerusalem shall be the centre of a world-wide kingdom, guarded by the presence of Jehovah Himself. In the picture of Joshua's trial we see the spiritual representative of the people first arraigned and then pardoned—an emblem of the change by which Zion's humiliation shall be turned into a condition of glory and favour (iii.). The golden candlestick is an emblem of the present power of the Spirit of God, as a source of grace and strength to the nation. The candlestick (*i.e.* the nation)

---

[1] It is noteworthy that there does not seem to be an actual *union in one person* of the offices of priest and king. Ch. vi. 13 speaks of a king and priest *sharing* a throne, sitting side by side. Between them will be the counsel of peace. Kirkpatrick takes *his* throne to mean *Jehovah's* throne. Cp. Pusey, *Minor Prophets*, p. 538, and Jerome quoted by him.

is fed by golden oil through the agency of heavenly ministers of grace (iv.). In spite of all obstacles, the temple shall yet be built, and the head-stone successfully laid. The next two visions typify the spiritual purgation of the restored people. The flying roll proclaims the extermination of sinners (v. 1-4). The vision of the woman in the ephah speaks of the taking away of sins,— the utter removal of iniquity (v. 5-11). Thus Israel is destined to become a *holy land* (ii. 12). The four chariots of the concluding vision are an emblem of judgment on the guilty world which has rejoiced over the suffering people of Jehovah (vi. 1-8 ; cp. Rev. xi.). The visions are closed by the description of the symbolic act already noticed, the solemn crowning of Joshua by the prophet (vi. 9 ff.).

The book of Zechariah marks what is in some respects a new departure in prophecy—or rather prophetic discourse assumes a new form. The direct address of Jehovah to the prophet is superseded by the *vision* ; that which was an occasional incident in the experience of earlier prophets becomes in Zechariah the normal method of divine teaching. Further, the prophet's relation to Jehovah is somewhat altered. The older prophets felt themselves to be in direct and living communion with God Himself; in the case of Zechariah it is an intermediary angel that instructs him in the purposes of God.

The seventh and eighth chapters represent a discourse delivered two years after the visions. Zechariah answers the inquiry, whether it was still obligatory to observe the fasts by which the Jews were accustomed to commemorate the destruction of Jerusalem. Zechariah's message is at once full of warning and of consolation. Sin had been the cause of Zion's rejection ; obedience would be followed by the restoration of Jerusalem as the spiritual metropolis of the world and the gathering of pilgrims from the heathen world, in order to share Israel's fellowship with her divine king (see viii. 20-23).

The preaching of Haggai and Zechariah was successful. It roused the nation to a sense of the importance of the work which they had allowed to lapse. The building of the temple was recommenced, and as the Persian satrap of the province, Tatnai, allowed the work to go on without interference, the temple was completed and dedicated in the year 516.

In some respects the writings of the two prophets, Haggai and Zechariah, show signs of declension in the gift of prophecy, and have rather the character of literary productions. Haggai's preaching is plain, simple, and unadorned; Zechariah's book seems not so much to embody personal preaching like that of the older prophets as to be the outcome of meditation and study. Nevertheless in some of their characteristics these two prophets are closely akin to their great predecessors. Thus both of them are persuaded that the Messianic age is close at hand, but that the divine promises to Israel are *conditional*, their fulfilment depending on the moral character of the restored exiles. Both prophets preach the need of mercy, justice, and righteousness in the ordinary dealings of civic and social life, and the future for which they look is one of spiritual renewal. Zechariah in particular predicts the abolition of wickedness, and the sanctification of Israel through the free outpouring of Jehovah's Spirit of grace (Zech. iii. 4; iv. 6; v. 5-11; viii. 16, 17). Again, though the visions of both prophets are to a great extent coloured by the religious revival of their day, and point to the exaltation of the temple and priesthood, their prophecies contain an element of true universalism. The second Isaiah's conception of Israel's special mission to the heathen world reappears in them. The heathen will be judged, but through judgment they will be brought to acknowledge Israel's God (Zech. viii. 20-23). The temple is to receive the offerings of the Gentiles (Hag. ii. 7; Zech. ii. 11; vi. 15; viii. 20 ff.); thither the desirable things of all nations shall be brought (Hag. ii. 7);[1] and Zion shall be the spiritual metropolis of the world. The thought of a Davidic king is not absent though it is kept in the background (see Hag. ii. 23; Zech. iii. 8).

Condition of the Jews between 516 and 458.—The half-

---

[1] Possibly this passage alludes to Isa. lx. 5 ff.

century which intervened between 516 and the mission of Ezra in 458, was one of grievous depression and disillusionment. The high and glowing anticipations of the prophets had pointed to the completion of the temple as the inauguration of Israel's Messianic age, but the external and internal conditions of the people became worse instead of better. Men were tempted to ask, Where are the promises made to the fathers? Moreover, Jehovah's requirements seemed oppressive; the service of the temple was a costly burden, and the daily restraints of the law seemed irksome. Hence many gave way to a temper of moroseness, indifference, and even hostility to God. They were tempted to fall back into heathen habits of thought and life; zeal for the maintenance of Israel's distinct and separate character as a people died down. The mood of the Jews at this period seems to be depicted in the book of Malachi, presently to be noticed; but one marked consequence of it may be gathered from the book of Ezra, viz. the general prevalence of mixed marriages—unions of Israelites with the half-breed 'people of the land,' alliances which were in many cases dictated by prudential and worldly motives. It is indeed possible that these mixed marriages represented something higher, namely a genuine desire on the part of the half-breeds to become full members of Jehovah's community, and a similar readiness on the part of some Jews to put the universalist aspirations of the prophets into practice. Nevertheless there was imminent danger of Judaism losing its proper character, and sinking back to the level of pre-exilic religion. For 'neither the inward nor the outward religion of that time was firmly enough established to assimilate without debasement or retrogression, a large influx of elements from a lower religious plane.'[1]

In order to understand the work of Ezra, it must be borne in mind that in opposition to the prevailing laxity, there was forming itself at this period a group of zealots, who clung the more closely to their religion as their

[1] Montefiore, *op. cit.* p. 303.

one consolation in these days of trial. They, like the *proud and evil doers* (Mal. ii. 17; iii. 15), but in a different temper of mind, were sensible of the apparent failure of Jehovah's promises; but instead of laying the blame on Jehovah and complaining of the hardness of His service and the heaviness of His yoke, they recognised in Israel itself the cause of the disappointment. It was Israel's faithlessness and indifference that now as of old hindered the accomplishment of the prophetic visions. The one hope of their fulfilment lay in a more strenuous and loyal observance on Israel's part of the moral conditions of Jehovah's covenant. It was this party—small indeed but resolute—which welcomed the mission of Ezra in 458. They felt that the restored exiles had much to learn from those who were still in Babylon. There a school had already formed itself on the basis of Ezekiel's teaching—a school which had devoted itself to the study, compilation, and transcription of the law, and whose peculiar view of the real gist and tendency of Israel's history is reflected in the priestly narrative of the Pentateuch and in the uniform tone of the historical books. Ezra's mission may have been dictated by a widespread anxiety among the Jews in Babylon, as to the religious condition of their compatriots in 'the province' (Neh. i. 3). **Ezra** himself was apparently a Zadokite, nearly related to the family of the high priest. He is also described as a scribe (Ezra vii. 6, etc.), a title which points to his having taken an active personal part in the codification and revision of the law. He received a commission from Artaxerxes Longimanus I., to *inquire concerning Judah and Jerusalem, according to the law of* his *God which was in his hand* (vii. 14-25).

Mission of Ezra, 458 B.C.—He came then to Jerusalem avowedly as a reformer, accompanied by a considerable company of more than 1000 persons. The object of his mission was to carry out a reform of the temple ceremonial on the basis of the new law-book, which was probably completed by about 500 B.C.[1] Ezra's first

---

[1] There is reason to think that this 'law-book' was substantially identical with the Pentateuch.

task, however, was that of dealing with the mixed marriages—an abuse of which he does not seem to have been fully aware till his arrival at Jerusalem. A struggle now began between the strict party, resolved under Ezra's leadership to put an end to the illegal marriages, and those, on the other hand, who were either hostile to reform on religious grounds, or were personally interested in upholding the *status quo*. It is obvious that a social reform of this kind was calculated to provoke a bitter and passionate resistance. An attempt of Ezra to rebuild the fortifications of Jerusalem failed owing to the intrigues of the neighbouring tribes, among whom there were doubtless individuals who felt personally aggrieved by Ezra's reformation. The result was that he lost his influence. For more than twelve years the party which supported him was compelled to remain inactive.

First visit of Nehemiah, 445.—In 445, however, it was reinforced and inspired with new hopes by the arrival of **Nehemiah**, who had obtained permission from Artaxerxes to visit his native city, ostensibly in order to repair the ruined walls and gates. By this time other serious social evils had arisen: the condition of the poorer Jews cried for redress; there were many practical grievances and abuses which demanded the prompt attention of the new governor. Further, the civil power represented by Nehemiah ranged itself on the side of the religious movement. Ezra now emerged from his retirement and reappeared upon the scene. In 444 a great assembly was held, in which the people bound themselves by a solemn oath to observe the statutes of the law. This occasion was the beginning of a determined effort to carry out the projected reform of Ezra, but the struggle was obstinate and the opposition was bitter. A certain number of malcontents even followed their wives into exile, and thus 'helped to kindle a flame of anger and revenge among the neighbouring communities, whose daughters had been exposed to indignity.'[1]

Judaism.—The movement we have briefly described

[1] Montefiore, *op. cit.* p. 310.

laid, as it were, the foundation-stone of post-exilic Judaism. The rigid race-separation of the Jew which made him hateful to all nations, and caused him to look down on all other religions as unclean and heathen, dates from this epoch. That proud scorn of the Gentile world, that fierce longing for the annihilation of Israel's enemies, which distinguishes some of the later literature of Judaism, may be said to have begun at this period. Humanly speaking, it was necessary that Jewish religion should pass through this stage, by which it was being providentially prepared for its struggle with Hellenism. After Alexander's death (323 B.C.) and the collapse of the Persian monarchy, Grecian influence became predominant in the East, and only one nation resisted the process of absorption and dissolution through which oriental thought and life became amalgamated with Greek culture and civilisation. The Jewish nation did not by any means escape the influence of the spirit of Hellenism, but it at least preserved what was peculiar and distinctive in its creed and habits of life. The law was a kind of coat-of-mail which enabled Judaism to present an impenetrable surface to the refined darts of Hellenism; it was a hard shell containing the precious kernel of a divine religion.[1]

Malachi, circ. 440.—The book of Malachi seems to belong to the period intervening between Nehemiah's first (445) and second visit (433). During his absence the abuses which Nehemiah had sternly repressed seem to have revived, and the two chief evils denounced by Malachi are those actually mentioned in Neh. xiii., viz. great negligence on the part of both priests and people in making provision for the temple-services, the payment of tithes, etc.; and the divorce of Israelitish wives and intermarriage with the heathen. (Cp. Mal. ii. 8-16 with Neh. xiii. 23-29; and Mal. iii. 8-10 with Neh. xiii. 10-12, 31.)

There is some reasonable doubt as to Malachi's personality. The name *Malachi*, 'My messenger' (cp. iii. 1) is very possibly not a proper name at all. In

---

[1] Cp. Cornill, *Der Israelitische Prophetismus*, p. 162.

the Septuagint version the heading of the book is *Oracle of the Word of the Lord against Israel by the hand of His messenger*; and the Targum adds the words 'whose name is called Ezra the scribe.' It is not improbable that the author of the book remained anonymous, and the compiler of the minor prophets may have prefixed to it a title taken from iii. 1.[1] Indeed, the words *The Burden of the Word of the Lord* point to a connection between three passages, viz. Zech. ix.-xi., Zech. xii.-xiv., and the book of Malachi. It has been supposed that these represent three anonymous prophetic writings which came into an editor's hands and were arranged in their present order at the close of the book of Zechariah. Some slight indication may be thus afforded of the true date of the last six chapters of Zechariah. In any case, there can be little question that the date traditionally assigned to the book of Malachi is correct.

The book itself is mainly a reproof grounded on the fact of Jehovah's unchanging love to Israel (i. 2-5). Jehovah had revealed Himself as the Father of His people (i. 6), and had entered into a covenant with Levi (ii. 4), but the priesthood had led the way in sinful neglect of the covenant conditions by contenting themselves with a perfunctory and grudging service of Jehovah. The earlier portion of the book (i. 6-ii. 9) accordingly contains a severe reproof addressed to the priests. There was a tendency among them to relax the observance of the Sabbath, and a growing disposition to look on the duties of the temple-service as monotonous taskwork. The worship of Jehovah seemed to be lost labour, since the yoke of the foreigner still pressed on Israel as heavily as before. The second portion of the book is addressed to the people (ii. 10 - iv. 6). The prophet specially denounces the sin of intermarriage with the heathen, and the perfidy with which divorce was resorted to (ii. 10-16). Malachi's message to the sceptical indifference and dull despondency of his contemporaries is that Jehovah shall suddenly appear as judge in the person of *the angel of the covenant* (iii. 1).

[1] Cp. Hag. i. 13.

That day will make manifest the distinction between the righteous and the sinner—between *him that serveth God and him that serveth Him not*. To Malachi, as to Haggai, the temple is the destined scene of this future theophany, and the main object of the divine judgment is to purify the sons of Levi, that there may once more be a faithful priesthood in Israel, and a pure offering acceptable to Jehovah (iii. 1-4).

Two things are specially noticeable in the teaching of this prophet. First, his style has a peculiar character. It is dialectical and didactic. He asks pointed questions, which he sometimes puts in the mouth of his hearers, and then gives a terse and abrupt answer of his own (*e.g.* i. 6, 7; ii. 17; iii. 13, 14). Further, he points the people to the law of Moses as supplying them with a disciplinary rule of life intended to prepare them for the day of Jehovah's coming. But Malachi's exaltation of the law, as constituting Israel's peculiar glory, is qualified by a touch of the older universalism. He probably felt that the rigid observance of Ezra's code was after all not an end but only a means, and that the aspirations of ancient prophecy pointed to a consummation wider and more satisfying than the mere triumph of Judaism. Thus in i. 11 he seems to teach that the true and acceptable worship of God might be independent of the temple; and the mention of *incense and a pure offering* (*Minchah*, 'vegetable offering') even points to the cessation of the sacrificial system of the law. Noteworthy also is Malachi's conception of the priestly function. He regards the priesthood mainly as a teaching office. Jehovah demands of His priests not merely personal sanctity. He requires that *the priest's lips should keep knowledge, and they should seek the law at his mouth; for he is the messenger of the Lord of hosts* (ii. 7).

Secondly, the teaching of Malachi is akin to that of earlier prophets in its ethical tone. It holds up before the people the moral conditions of acceptance with Jehovah. The very conception of the advent of the angel of the covenant for the purpose of a sifting and searching judgment implies that Israel's sin is the cause of its present tribulation. The passage iii. 5 is entirely in the manner of the older prophets: *I will come near to you to judgment, and I will be a swift witness against the sorcerers and against the adulterers and against false swearers and against those that oppress the hireling in his wages, the widow and the fatherless, and that turn aside the stranger from his right, and fear not me, saith the Lord of hosts.* Again, the call to repentance with which the book concludes recalls the characteristics of pre-exilic prophecy. The predicted appearance of Elijah is intended to prepare the people by penitence for the advent of Jehovah Himself, whose visitation of an impenitent nation must necessarily bring not a blessing but a curse (iv. 4-6).

CHAPTER VI

LATER POST-EXILIC PROPHECY

The century of Jewish history which followed Nehemiah's work at Jerusalem, and which, roughly speaking, closes with the death of Alexander (323), is one of which we know but little. It is certain, however, that a literary process of expansion and redaction was being applied to the writings of the prophets. As we have already noticed, fragments of prophecy were carefully collected and inserted in one or other of the four books of the prophets. There is little reason to doubt that editorial additions were occasionally made. It has been supposed, for example, that the striking homily on fasting, which forms the fifty-eighth chapter of Isaiah, is an instance of such expansion. Such additions would, as a rule, deal with the Messianic expectations of Israel, depicting the age of the Messiah in one or other of its generally recognised aspects. But the general character of Judaistic writings is as might be expected nationalistic, representing Israel as relatively righteous, and the heathen as objects of divine vengeance. The intention of these passages is to console Israel rather than to reprove it, and to sustain it by predictions of overwhelming judgments on the nations which had either actually oppressed the chosen people or had menaced its tranquillity.

Apocalyptic literature.—It is necessarily somewhat uncertain what parts of four books of the 'prophets' are to be attributed to this period;[1] but one indication of date is to be found in the fact that some of the later writings are of an apocalyptic type, dealing with the

[1] Possibly Isa. xi. 10-16; xxiv.-xxvii.; xxxii.-xxxiii.; lxiii.-lxvi.; Jer. l., li.; Zech. xii.-xiv., belong to this group of writings.

distant future rather than with the conditions of the present; with the fortunes of Israel and the prospects of the divine kingdom in its relation to the world rather than with the personal glories of the promised Messiah. Apocalyptic literature is in fact specially characteristic of Judaism, just as prophecy is of pre-exilic religion, and the vision of Ezekiel, which concludes his book, forms perhaps a kind of connecting link between prophecy and apocalypse. The most indisputable specimen in the Old Testament of an apocalyptic book is the book of **Daniel**, but some of the peculiar features of this type of literature already appear (*a*) in the last six chapters of Zechariah; (*b*) in the books of Joel and Obadiah, and (*c*) in the fragment which forms Isaiah xxiv.-xxvii.

Zechariah ix.-xiv.—(*a*) The last six chapters of the book of Zechariah are wholly distinct in style and tone from the admitted work of that prophet. There is still a great conflict of opinion respecting their date: some, like Schultz, regarding them as belonging to the eighth or seventh century B.C., others, like Cornill, placing them as late as the time of Alexander, towards the close of the fourth century. Possibly their position in the canon between Zechariah and Malachi corresponds to a well-grounded tradition respecting their date, but the point in any case is not of crucial importance.[1] Dr. Driver's conclusion probably represents the utmost we can safely maintain in the present state of our knowledge. 'Perhaps we may be justified in concluding . . . that the prophecy as a whole dates from the eighth century B.C., but that it was modified in details, and accommodated to a later situation by a prophet[2] living in the post-exilic

[1] Bennett, *Primer of the Bible*, p. 114. 'The history of these prophecies is probably similar to that of Isaiah xl.-lxvi. The writings of Zechariah closed the volume of the minor prophets, and the two anonymous works, Zech. ix.-xiv., and the book of Malachi, were added as appendices, and the absence of any name in the heading, ix. 1, led to ix.-xiv. being considered an integral part of the book of Zechariah.'

[2] Or possibly two prophets, one the author of ix.-xi., the other the author of xii.-xiv. See Driver's *Introduction* (ed. 1), p. 328. In ed. 6, p. 349, Dr. Driver very slightly modifies his former view.

period when the Greeks had become formidable to the Jews and many Jews had been exiled among them.' We seem thus to be justified in regarding Zech. ix.-xiv. as a specimen of that expansion of prophecy which we have already noticed; it combines some features of pre-exilic writings with distinct characteristics of a late post-exilic age. In these chapters four main subjects may be distinguished :—

(1) *The advent of Messiah.* In ix. x. the author describes the progress of a purifying judgment through the Holy Land, destroying the nations (heathen) who dwell in it, or reducing them to dependence and subjection. Thus the way is prepared for the king Messiah, who is welcomed to Zion, destroys the weapons of war, proclaims peace, and reigns over the land. In virtue of the covenant sealed by blood (Exod. xxiv. 8) Zion's children have already been restored from the dungeon of exile; those who are still waiting for release are invited to return (ix. 11-12). But peace and plenty are only restored through conflict; Judah is Jehovah's bow, Ephraim His arrow, Zion His sword, her sons His spear (ix. 13). Jehovah is the hope of His land; not the idols or diviners through whom Zion has become an unshepherded flock, and has fallen into the hands of false shepherds (x. 1, 2). Jehovah will substitute new rulers for these unworthy shepherds, and Judah now united to Ephraim will gain a decisive victory over its foes; Egypt and Asshur will be humiliated.

Here the main idea is that of Messiah's advent as a prince of peace, righteous and victorious over Israel's foes. But this conception is qualified by the hint in ix. 9, 10. The king is victorious (lit. *delivered*; cp. 1 Sam. xiv. 45) but lowly. Thus the thought is suggested of a prince triumphant through humiliation. The exilic picture of the suffering servant of Jehovah has so far modified the ancient presentment of the Messianic king.

(2) In xi. we have an allegory that might be entitled 'the rejected shepherd.' A hostile invasion of Palestine takes place from the north filling the unworthy shepherds (rulers) with dismay. The prophet himself, representing Jehovah, undertakes the care of the people

—*the flock of slaughter*, *i.e.* the flock neglected and maltreated by its proper rulers. He assumes as emblems of his office two staves, called 'graciousness' and 'union' (in reference to Jehovah's goodness and the union of Judah with Israel). He deposes the evil rulers, but his authority is ungratefully repudiated by the people. They give him for his wage a paltry sum—the price of a slave. In token that he is God's representative he places the money in the temple treasury, and solemnly breaks his staves in order to show that the divine protection is at end, and that the union of Israel with Judah is dissolved. The prophet then assumes the character of a *foolish shepherd*, *i.e.* a hard and merciless ruler, who makes havoc of the people; but he himself is finally smitten by the sword and the flock dispersed. Only a third part remains to constitute the faithful people of God (xiii. 9).[1]

There seems to lie behind these passages the well-known prophecies of Jeremiah xxiii. 1-8, and of Ezekiel xxxiv. It is a solemn warning of the way in which divine grace may be frustrated by human obstinacy. The truth which it conveys had been abundantly illustrated in the past history of Israel. It was to receive a more terrible illustration in the subsequent history of the nation.[2]

(3) *The restoration and penitence of the people* (xii.-xiv.). Here the writer evidently recalls the prophecies of Ezekiel, relating to the attack of the nations on Jerusalem (Ezek. xxxviii. and xxxix.). The prophet in xii. sees an assault of the nations upon Jerusalem. Among her foes is mentioned *Judah* (xii. 1-3). These are however stricken with panic, and the chiefs of Judah, seeing that Jehovah fights for His own city, come to Jerusalem's aid. Jehovah Himself then delivers both Judah and Jerusalem. But the day of deliverance is also a day of mourning (xii. 10). On the inhabitants of Jerusalem is poured out *the Spirit of grace and of supplication*. A general lamentation takes place; a fountain is opened for the purgation of sin and of uncleanness; the idols are cut off, and prophets cease out of the land, the pretension to be a prophet being

---

[1] The passage xiii. 7-9 must be closely connected with xi. from which it has become somehow detached.
[2] Kirkpatrick, *op. cit.* p. 465.

for some reason regarded as no longer honourable. The clue to this picture of repentance is perhaps supplied by xiii. 7-9, a passage which seems to suggest that the penitence of the people is occasioned by some unjust deed of blood of which they have been guilty.

(4) In xiv. *the final assault of the heathen* on Jerusalem is described. The nations capture the holy city and carry half of its inhabitants into captivity. Jehovah appears in order to provide a way of escape for the remainder, and the Messianic age thereupon begins. Two streams issue forth from Jerusalem to fertilise the land (8-11). The city itself is rebuilt, and a desolating and terrible judgment falls upon the heathen nations. Those who escape join with Jehovah's people in doing homage to Him at the feast of tabernacles. The vision ends with the picture of a city wholly consecrated to Jehovah's service. This nationalistic representation of the Messianic age is obviously characteristic of Judaism; we note especially the exaltation and increased importance of the capital, and the vehement hatred of the heathen. The universalism of the earlier prophets reappears in the predictions pointing to the ultimate triumph of Judaism, and the incorporation of the heathen into the kingdom of God as fellow-worshippers of Jehovah in the mode characteristic of Israel itself.

In the last chapter it will be pointed out what important elements the concluding part of the book of Zechariah contributes to the Messianic idea. It is only necessary here to note that in its present shape this section of the 'Prophets' is Judaistic in tone rather than Hebraistic.

Joel, circ. 350.—(*b*) We now come to the book of **Joel**, with regard to which there is much uncertainty. The choice lies between assigning to it a very early date, *e.g.* the early part of the reign of Joash, before Syria or Assyria had become formidable (circ. 837-817); or the period between Ezra's work at Jerusalem and the death of Alexander. On the whole the considerations in favour of this later date preponderate, as there are several features of the book characteristic of Judaism rather than of pre-exilic prophecy, *e.g.* the absence of any mention of the northern kingdom, the reference to ceremonial and hierarchical ideas, the prediction of vengeance upon the heathen, and, above all, the absence of reproofs. The prophet speaks of Israel as if it were relatively righteous in the eyes of Jehovah, and herein the book presents a marked contrast to the writings of early prophets, such as Hosea and Amos. It is on the whole the most reasonable view that Joel combines many elements derived from the older prophecy,[1] but in many of its characteristics the book appears to resemble the apocalyptic literature. The occasion of Joel's prophecy seems to have been an unprecedented plague of locusts, accompanied by a severe drought. This terrible visitation prefigures the advent of the great *Day of the Lord*, which in earlier prophets had been so prominent a theme. The actual circumstances of the visitation are regarded by the prophet as typical. The locust army destroyed is a type of hostile nations repelled; the return of the rain is a symbol of the outpouring of the Spirit; the present temporal deliverance is a proof of Jehovah's favour towards His people (ii. 27), and a pledge of that perpetual divine indwelling which is the climax of blessing (iii. 21). An indication of late date is Joel's distinction between Israel and the nations. The day of Jehovah is not regarded by him as a day of moral sifting for Israel itself, but as a day in which the nations shall be judged and Israel saved and blessed. 'The nations are judged for the wrongs done by them to Israel; they have no share in the blessings of the future; the outpouring of the Spirit is limited to Israel; deliverance is promised only to Jerusalem and to those found there.'[2]

The following then are the leading ideas of Joel:—

(1) *The day of the Lord* is regarded in its twofold aspect as a day of terror yet of blessing, of judgment yet of salvation. The coming of the plague marks the dawn of that awful day. The visitation, it should be observed, is somewhat idealised and probably points back to the plague of locusts in Egypt. Joel's locusts are 'the prototype of the apocalyptic locusts of Rev. ix. 3-10.'

(2) *The outpouring of the Spirit*, the spiritual blessing

---

[1] See Driver, *Introduction*, p. 311.
[2] Driver, *The Book of Joel*, p. 32.

being suggested by the promise of a lower blessing, rain and harvest. Joel is the 'Old Testament prophet of the Holy Ghost.'[1]

(3) The counterpart of the blessing outpoured on Israel is the *judgment upon the nations*. Joel predicts a great judicial act whereby Israel is to be finally delivered from its foes. There is no hint even such as closed Zech. xiv., that the nations will one day be gathered into Jehovah's kingdom, and share the privileges and blessings of His covenant. Nevertheless Joel differs from the later apocalyptic writers in the fact that there are no 'exaggerated national pretensions' in his book. The Israel of the future, upon which the divine blessings are destined to descend, is the present Israel spiritually transformed (ii. 28) and *calling upon* Jehovah in faithfulness (ii. 32). On the other hand, in his earnest call to repentance, in the invitation to *return to Jehovah*, Joel is in line with the older prophets, while his prophecy of an indwelling of Jehovah in the midst of His renewed people, and of an outpouring of the Spirit, suggest a connection between his book and the great visions of Ezekiel and the later Isaiah. Probably he owes his position among the prophets to the fact that Joel iii. 16 is apparently repeated from Amos i. 2; and that the *Day of the Lord* is so prominent a theme in his book (cp. Amos v. 18).

Obadiah.—As in the case of Joel, so in that of **Obadiah**, a book of similar tendency, the question of date is uncertain. The settlement of this point mainly turns upon the relation of Obadiah to Jeremiah xlix. 7-22. But the general standpoint in regard to *the nations*, which are objects of judgment not of grace, may betoken either an early or late date. The day of distress mentioned in Obad. 11-14 may have been the destruction of the city and temple by the Chaldæans in 586;[2] or it may have been some earlier occasion, such as the capture of the city by united bands of Philistines and Arabs in Jehoram's reign (848-844) described in 2 Chron. xxi. 16, 17. There seems to be one verse of Joel (ii. 32), which makes a

[1] *Obs.* the words *all flesh* (in ii. 28) are limited by the context to Israel's sons and daughters.
[2] Cp. Ps. cxxxvii. 7.

distinct reference to Obadiah 17. If he is post-exilic he cannot have been later than Joel. In any case the terms used of Edom's conduct by Obadiah seem to be too strong to refer to any mere predatory excursion. On the whole it seems best to treat the question of date as entirely open; but the indications are in favour of the conclusion that the book, in its present form, while it incorporates earlier elements, belongs to the post-exilic period, when the former fate of Edom was perhaps commonly regarded as 'an episode in Jehovah's judgment on the heathen generally.'[1]

In the book of Obadiah then, the special foe of Israel is Edom. The offence of Edom was aggravated by the nearness of its kinship to Israel. Edom was the descendant of Esau, Jacob's brother, 'Loud and long has been the wail of execration which has gone up from the Jewish nation against Edom. It is the one imprecation which breaks forth from the Lamentations of Jeremiah ... it is the bitterest drop in the sad recollections of the Israelite captives by the waters of Babylon.'[2] In Obadiah's prophecy, however, Edom seems to be taken as the representative of the whole heathen world regarded as hostile to God's kingdom. The later Jews understood Edom in Ps. cxxxvii. to mean Pagan Rome; others found in 'Edom' a mystical designation of the Christians, 'the Nazarene people who are of the sons of Edom, whose beginning and origin is the city of Rome.'[3]

The object of Obadiah's book is to denounce the pride and malignity of Edom, and to predict the judgment about to descend on it and on *all the nations* (Obad. 15). In the great *day of Jehovah* the one hope of salvation will be on mount Zion. Hebrew captives will be restored to their home, and Jehovah's kingdom shall be finally established. Deliverers[4] will come up on mount Zion who *shall judge the mount of Esau* (21).

[1] So Wellhausen; see Driver, *Introduction* (ed. 6), p. 321.
[2] Stanley, *The Jewish Church*, vol. ii. p. 556. See Lam. iv. 21, 22; Ps. cxxxvii. 7. See also Ezek. xxv. 8, 12-14; Jer. xlix. 7-22; Isa. lxiii. 1-4.
[3] Abarbanel, *Com. on Obad.*, cp. Perowne on Ps. cxxxvii. 7.
[4] This term recalls the Judges (Judg. iii. 9, 15; Neh. ix. 27); but LXX. has ἄνδρες σεσωσμένοι. Heb. מוֹשִׁיעִים.

Isaiah xxiv.-xxvii. circ. 330.—It has been surmised that the splendid passage Isa. xxiv.-xxvii., which closes the series of prophecies against the nations, was occasioned by the fall of the Persian empire before the arms of Alexander. Its subject is the general judgment upon the world and its inhabitants. The prophecy evidently partakes of an ideal and apocalyptic character, describing not merely the judgment that descends upon this or that oppressive power, but the final ruin of the world-power. The scene of ruin alternates with the triumph-songs of the redeemed. The hostile power is alluded to as a great city (xxv. 2, 3; xxvi. 5), and its overthrow as the work of Jehovah Himself, not of the Messianic king. Israel takes no part in the conquest. It is enjoined as of old to *stand still and see the salvation of Jehovah* (Exod. xiv. 13). *Come, my people, enter thou into thy chambers and shut thy doors about thee; hide thyself for a little moment until the indignation be overpast. For behold, Jehovah cometh out of his place to punish the inhabitants of the earth for their iniquity: the earth also shall disclose her blood and shall no more cover her slain* (Isa. xxvi. 20, 21). The goal of history is conceived as a reign of Jehovah on mount Zion, a heavenly feast, and a removal of *the veil spread over all nations* (xxv. 6, 7). Only Moab is excluded from the salvation which is extended to all other peoples. For individual Israelites there is a hope held out of a resurrection from the dead. The idea of a resurrection of Israel *as a nation* from its grave is found already in Hosea (vi. 2; xiii. 14), and Ezekiel (xxxvii.). The divine victory over death of which the prophet speaks in Isa. xxvi., includes the awakening to new life of the *godly members* of the elect nation who have perished. A quickening dew falls from heaven on the bones of them who dwell in dust. The earth yields up her dead, and no more covers her slain (Isa. xxvi. 19-21).

Jonah.—There remains yet another book which is included among the minor prophets, but which has peculiar and special characteristics. The book of Jonah is not a book of prophecy in the same sense as the other writings we have considered. It narrates a particular passage in the life of one of the very earliest prophets, Jonah,

the son of Amittai, who is mentioned in 2 Kings
xiv. 25 as having exercised his ministry in the days
of Jeroboam II. He seems to have predicted that great
extension of the boundaries of the northern kingdom
which actually took place during the reign of the last
king of Jehu's dynasty. According to a Jewish tradition,
Jonah was the son of the widow of Zarephath, who
was recalled to life by Elijah (1 Kings xvii.), and his
birthplace is said to have been Gath-Hepher, in Zebulun
(2 Kings xiv. 25). The original prophecies of Jonah
are not extant, but the book which is ascribed to him,
or rather of which he is the hero, relates an epoch-
making incident in Israel's history—the preaching of
the gospel of repentance to a great heathen nation.

The nature of the book is noticeable. It is a narrative
of much the same kind as those which relate to Elijah
and Elisha in the two books of Kings. The miraculous
element in it is twofold. First, there is Jonah's own
marvellous preservation from death in the belly of the
great fish by which he is swallowed. Again, there is
the rapid growth of the gourd, or *palma Christi*, under
which the prophet shelters himself from the fierce heat
of the midday sun. There is also the moral miracle of
a huge population being brought by a kind of spon-
taneous impulse to repentance and amendment. It is
possible that there were traditions of Jonah's history
which supplied a basis of fact for the story contained
in the book. For instance, it is quite possible that
Jonah was actually sent to preach at Nineveh after
some wonderful deliverance from death which made his
appearance a sign to the Ninevites (St. Matt. xii. 39).
Nor is there any *a priori* difficulty in supposing that a
notable miracle may have marked the important crisis
in the history of redemption which the mission of Jonah
implies. On the contrary, every such new beginning
in Old Testament history seems to be signalised by
the occurrence of miracles. But there are very strong
reasons for believing that the writer of the book lived
several centuries after the death of Jonah, and that
the story is to be regarded as a narrative written with
didactic intention; in other words, that it is a story

THE BOOK OF JONAH

intended to convey a moral. A close examination of the book has led most modern critics to declare with confidence that it is a post-exilic work, very probably composed at some time during the fifth, or possibly the fourth century, B.C., *i.e.* during the very period when Israel was going through that process of rigid self-separation from the heathen world which was indeed a necessary stage in its spiritual education, but which was very possibly carried out with indiscriminate and sometimes exaggerated zeal. The book seems to have been written with the design of correcting the narrow, exclusive, 'particularist' idea that the sphere of salvation and grace was confined to Israel alone. Jonah's reluctance to preach at Nineveh, and his anger at its repentance, reflects the usual attitude of Judaism towards the heathen world.[1] Jonah represents the characteristic Jewish temper which Tacitus describes in the sentence, *Adversus omnes alios hostile odium* (*Hist.* v. 5). Already in Jeremiah xviii. 7 ff. there is a tacit protest against this temper; the prophet there teaches that repentance might avert punishment even in the case of the heathen nations. The mission of Jonah illustrates Jeremiah's teaching, and somewhat extends it. For its last word is a message of the creative compassion of God for all that He has made, the mercy which extends over all His works.

Accordingly, we should observe the *evangelic purport* of the book. Whenever God brought Israel into relation with any heathen peoples He made Himself known to them: to Egypt He manifested Himself through Joseph and Moses, to Philistia in the capture of the Ark, to Syria through Elisha, to Babylon through Daniel, to Persia through Esther. It is the teaching of Jonah that God is more merciful than man, and that the work of taking vengeance upon Israel's foes is not so dear to Him as that of bringing all men everywhere to repentance and salvation. A noble spirit of universalism appears in the book. The conduct of the Ninevites is perhaps intentionally made to contrast

---

[1] Cp. Acts xiii. 45; 1 Thess. ii. 16.

favourably with that of the prophet fleeing from the voice of Jehovah; and the behaviour of the heathen sailors on board Jonah's ship is marked by natural humanity. Further, the hated 'nations' are seen to be capable of responding to divine grace, and to be objects of divine mercy. Again, we should notice *the typical character* of the book. Jonah is at once a true representative of the people to which he belonged, and a type of Jesus Christ. The narrow-heartedness of the prophet makes him a type of his people. His story illustrates the truth that 'the self-will and transgression of an actual individual may be the most complete of all parables to illustrate the self-will and transgressions of his class or nation.'[1] Hence the whole book may be looked on as an allegory, in which God's purpose for Israel is prefigured. Like Jonah, Israel was designed by God to be the prophet of the nations, and the light of the Gentiles (Isa. xlii. 6). Like Jonah, Israel was removed from its own land and cast into the great sea of nations which encircled it; it was, as it were, swallowed up by the great world-power of Babylon. It is noteworthy that Jeremiah li. 34 does, in fact, employ this very image in describing the captivity.[2] Like Jonah, Israel in its affliction turns to God in penitence. Like Jonah, it is restored to life (cp. Ezek. xxxvii.), and then longs to see vengeance wreaked upon its heathen foes, and murmurs because the judgment is delayed. No one can deny that the lesson of the book of Jonah was much needed after the exile. The thought with which it closes is indeed from some points of view the most sublime in the Old Testament. It carries the revelation of Israel's God to a point only one step removed from the teaching of the New Testament.

[1] Maurice, *Prophets and Kings of the Old Testament*, p. 354.
[2] On 'The great fish and what it means' see the admirable chapter in Dr. G. A. Smith's *The Book of the Twelve Prophets*, vol. ii. p. 523. Dr. Smith proves convincingly that the writer of Jonah employs a familiar image supplied by the popular mythology of ancient Palestine, traces of which may be discerned in other parts of Scripture: *e.g.* Job iii. 8, vii. 12, xxvi. 12, 13; Ps. lxxiv. 14; Isa. xxvii. 1, li. 9, and especially Jerem. li. 34, 44.

JONAH A TYPE OF CHRIST

It speaks of Jehovah as not only the national Deity of a single people, but as the God and Father of the whole world, whose mercy is over all His works, and to whom man as such, man created in His own image, is precious. The last note of prophecy is thus the note of divine love, 'We are left with this grand vague vision of the immeasurable city [1] with its multitude of innocent children and cattle, and God's compassion brooding over all.'

On the other hand, God's dealings with the prophet make him a type of Jesus Christ. His fate is prophetic. He is cast out as a propitiatory victim, is restored to life, and becomes a preacher of peace to the heathen. In His reference to the book (St. Matt. xii. 39), our blessed Lord deals with the story of Jonah rather as a prophecy than as literal history. He sets His seal to the spirit and tendency of the book, but His allusion does not in any sense determine its precise literary character. We shall best recognise the true import and tendency of the book, and its bearing on our Lord's atoning work, by careful consideration of such passages as St. Matt. xii. 39; St. Luke xi. 29, and especially St. John xii. 32. With the book of Jonah the prophetic literature of Israel may be said to close, for the book of Daniel, next to be considered, is not classed by the Jews among the prophets. It is inserted among the 'Hagiographa,' a fact which at once indicates a comparatively late date, and discriminates the book from those of the 'Prophets' already considered.

The Book of Daniel, circ. 165.—The book of Daniel seems indeed to be a book of consolation addressed to the confessors and martyrs who suffered during the persecution of Antiochus Epiphanes. The book reflects the conditions of the last and most significant crisis in the history of Old Testament religion, when it was fighting a life-and-death struggle with Hellenism.

---

[1] G. A. Smith, *op. cit.*, p. 541. Incidentally Professor Smith points out that Nineveh, 'the great city,' must have long ceased to be what it was before its fall in 606. Its greatness had become 'a matter of tradition' when the author of Jonah wrote.

104   THE BOOK OF DANIEL

After the division of Alexander's empire, Palestine remained for upwards of a century an Egyptian province. During this period the Jews enjoyed comparative tranquillity under the mild and wise rule of the Ptolemies. In 198 however Antiochus the Great annexed Phœnicia and Palestine to the kingdom of Syria. Antiochus IV. (Epiphanes), who succeeded to the throne in 175, had been brought up at Rome, where he had imbibed a strong contempt for the religion and peculiar customs of the Jews. Accordingly he at first actively favoured the Hellenising party in Judæa, and ultimately made a determined effort to abolish Judaism by force. He polluted the temple and the altar with swine's flesh, forced the Jews to take part in heathen rites, destroyed all copies of the Law on which he could lay his hands, and carried on a relentless persecution against all who still held fast to the sacred rites of their religion. A desperate struggle for freedom began under the leadership of the sons of the priest Mattathias, of whom Judas Maccabæus was the most prominent. The struggle was ultimately successful. In 165 Antiochus died, and in the same year the daily sacrifice was restored at Jerusalem. Thus the Jews emerged from their terrible ordeal with their religious independence restored under the leadership of the family of the Maccabees. It was seemingly at the height of the struggle in the year 165 or 164 that the book of Daniel was written.

The design of the unknown writer of Daniel is to comfort his suffering compatriots and nerve them for their conflict by a book which is of an apocalyptic rather than a prophetic character. By study, by calculation of dates, by comparison of ancient predictions, the apocalyptic writer sought to discover some clue to the drift of present events, and the probable developments of the future. Nevertheless it is probable that the book of Daniel rests upon a traditional basis, and that the writer availed himself of some work or works dealing with the history of Babylon in the sixth century B.C.

The book of Daniel differs from the earlier prophetic literature chiefly in the circumstance that its outlook is wider and more comprehensive. It is the first attempt at a philosophy of history. 'It is dominated by an overmastering sense of a universal divine purpose which overrules all the vicissitudes of human history, the rise and fall of dynasties, the conflicts of nations, and the calamities that overtake the faithful.'[1] Indeed the circumstances of their later history forced the Jews to face the question, How long that heathen domination, from which they seemed destined never to escape, was likely to last. The writer of Daniel surveys the future history of the elect people in its relation to the kingdoms of the world, and depicts in glowing colours the final deliverance of *the saints*. He is akin to the ancient prophets in his sense of God's control and ordering of history, and in his conception of salvation as a certain blessing of the future. He differs from them in his free use of symbolic imagery, and in certain theological ideas which point to a late date. For instance, the book illustrates some characteristic religious practices of later Judaism: *e.g.* its fervour in fasting and prayer, and its growing tendency to exalt the merit of almsgiving.

It has been said that the teaching of the Old Testament is summed up in one word—the word GOD. It is in their persistent witness to the nature and requirement of God that all the prophetical and quasi-prophetical books of the Old Testament are united. It is true that in the latest books, the spirit of Jewish nationalism makes its appearance; but the splendid visions of Israel's future presuppose an inward purification and renewal of the nation itself. It is the righteous, and they only, who are destined to behold the glory of God, and to inherit the blessings of the Messianic kingdom. Penitence, faith, loyalty to the divinely-revealed law—these are the essential conditions of acceptance with God, inculcated alike by Isaiah and Ezekiel, by Hosea and by Daniel. Thus the goodly fellowship of the prophets with one voice proclaims that *the righteous Lord loveth righteousness,* and that the moral law is the chief link between the soul of man and God.

[1] *Bampton Lectures,* 1897, p. 332.

CHAPTER VII

THE MESSIANIC HOPE

As we have seen, prediction is by no means the most essential element in prophecy. The prophet was above all else a preacher of righteousness to the men of his own day. His teaching was rooted in present experience and dealt with moral questions of present urgency. His visions of the future were likewise coloured by the facts of the present. 'The prophetic oracles were addressed to the present, were rooted in the present, were expressed in language suited to the present, and pointed to a good in the near future forming a counterpart to present evil, or to an evil in the near future which was to be the penalty of present and past sin.'[1] Nevertheless, it remains true that inspired prophecy ever points to a future time, when the great principles which it had discerned to be at work in Israel's history, would be openly manifested and developed. From first to last the prophets of the Old Testament look and wait for a *Kingdom of God*; they depict its nature and conditions in varied and many-sided imagery; they point with ever-increasing clearness to a personal Being, in whom and by whom all the types, figures and anticipations of the old dispensation will be brought to fulfilment. Thus, the Messianic doctrine of the prophets is best understood if studied in close connection with the history of their times; and we must ever bear in mind that they spoke under limitations of which they were, to some extent, conscious (1 Pet. i. 11). The result is that we discover in Christianity not so much the literal accomplishment of particular predictions

---

[1] Bruce, *The Chief End of Revelation*, p. 221.

EARLY PREDICTIONS 107

as a broad but close correspondence between Messianic prediction in general, and its spiritual fulfilment in Christ. This concluding chapter will be devoted to a brief sketch of the growth of the Messianic hope during the period covered by the prophetic literature.

Early stages in Messianic prediction.—It is necessary to remember at the outset that there already existed spiritual hopes which the prophets inherited. The primaeval promise to Abraham (Gen. xxii. 18) was doubtless an ancient and cherished tradition (Mic. vii. 20). The earliest stage of the Messianic expectation was a belief in man's *dominion*, and his destined victory over evil (Gen. iii. 15). This took more definite shape in the promise that in Abraham and his seed all the inhabitants of the world should be blessed (Gen. xxii. 17, 18). The so-called 'Blessing of Jacob' (Gen. xlix.) which is probably a primitive ode composed of different tribal songs or proverbs, and which perhaps originally formed part of an ancient collection of national poetry, exalts the figure of Judah as the future holder of sovereignty over his people. Judah is depicted as a judge or ruler with the staff of office in his hand, exercising in his own right the sovereignty which was the promised heritage of Abraham's descendants. The prediction ascribed to Balaam (Num. xxiv. 17), hints at the sway of an individual, which is to proceed from Israel and to be ultimately extended over the other nations of the East. Israel's deliverance from the bondage of Egypt and its experiences in the wilderness had already indeed suggested certain ideas which later prophecy develops. For instance, the foundation of the notion of a visible *kingdom of God* was laid in the primitive polity organised by Moses; the thought of triumph over heathen enemies by an elect people separated to Jehovah's service was a natural result of the discomfiture of Egypt and of Amalek. The promulgation of the Law on Sinai indicated that the future pre-eminence of Israel would be a spiritual rather than a physical fact, and would depend on ethical conditions. At the same time, the judgments which descended on Israel's enemies were already seen to be successive declarations in regard to the divine estimate of human sin. Finally, Moses himself was a typical figure. His commanding and authoritative position in Israel indicated the principle that the divine guidance of Israel was, and would continue to be, direct but *mediatorial*. It is true that the promise of Deut. xviii. 15 is not expressly connected with the person of the Messiah anywhere in the Old Testament,[1] but towards the period of the close of the canon, the expectation of a coming prophet seems to have revived (see Mal. iv. 5; cp. 1 Macc. xiv. 41).

Reign of David, circ. 1010-978.—The reign of David gave a direction and impulse to the Messianic idea which was never afterwards lost. It manifested the compatibility of a human hereditary monarchy with the fact of a divinely-ruled polity. In David the hopes of Israel were centred, as in one who had been chosen by God to fulfil and realise in his own person the ideal of theocratic sovereignty. David himself seems to have been conscious of a unique vocation (Ps. xviii., 2 Sam. xxiii. 1-8) and of a promise of divine favour pledged to his house for evermore.

2 Sam. vii. 4 ff.—The oracle of Nathan (2 Sam. vii. 4 ff.) seems to embody the hopes which the men of David's own generation connected with his name and family. It predicts the everlasting continuance of David's throne and house; it bestows on the theocratic king the dignity of divine *sonship*. Thus, long before the earliest of the eighth-century prophets appeared, popular tradition already ascribed an ideal glory and greatness to David's house. David's reign was commonly regarded as the pattern of Messianic times, a kind of golden age in Israel's history which was destined to be restored in the future. In the light of this promise to David's house, each king who sits on the throne of Judah is transfigured and invested with more than human attributes, whether he is hailed as a victorious warrior (Ps. ii.), or as a royal bridegroom taking to himself a consort from the heathen world (Ps. xlv.), as a monarch reigning in righteousness and peace (Ps. lxxii.), or finally, as one who combines the

---

[1] This passage primarily refers to a continuous *line* of prophets, through whom Jehovah from time to time manifests His Will.

functions of royalty with those of priesthood (Ps. cx.),—the promised dignity of the Davidic prince with the prerogatives of the ancient king who had blessed the patriarch Abraham himself (Gen. xiv. 19). Thus the figure of David loomed large in the imagination of the people at the period when written prophecy began. In the eighth century B.C., when the huge empire of Assyria threatened Israel's very existence as a nation, faith clung to the covenant established by Jehovah with David and his house.

It is accordingly not a matter of surprise that in the earliest prophetic writings a frequent Messianic vision is that of a royal personage, in and through whom Israel is to find deliverance from its foes. The world-power attacked the theocracy specially in the person of its monarch, and naturally enough the figure of the king became more and more the centre of Israel's hopes; in allegiance to David's house alone would there be any prospect of salvation for the hardly-pressed northern kingdom.

The Davidic King.—The predictions of a Davidic king reach their climax on the very eve of the struggle with Assyria, in the prophecies of Micah and Isaiah. Prophecy now declares that the future king is to come from David's own city (Mic. v. 2; cp. Matt. ii. 6), and is to stand and feed his flock in Jehovah's name (Mic. v. 4). In other words he is destined to stand in a unique relation to God, gifted with His Spirit (Isa. xi. 1), executing His righteous purpose, guided by His wisdom, even acting as the medium of His self-revelation (Isa. ix. 6). His chosen city, Jerusalem, is to be the metropolis of nations; His throne will be everlasting and His people holy (Isa. iv. 3). In all these representations we may discern a two-fold aspect of sovereignty. On the one hand, since David was a typical man of war (1 Chron. xxviii. 3), the Messianic ideal necessarily included the thought of victory and triumph over foes. The title of 'king' was essentially that of a warrior, a leader of hosts in *the wars of the Lord*. It was a pledge not only of the deliverance of Israel from its enemies, but of a perpetual extension of the visible boundaries of the theocratic kingdom.

This aspect however of the Messianic character, was not perhaps the most prominent. The world-wide conquests of the Davidic king were destined only to form the prelude to a peaceful rule. The advance of the Assyrian power no doubt gave a stimulus to universalistic ideas, to the conception of a world-monarchy extended by warlike prowess; but the permanent form of Messianic prediction was mainly determined by visions of a stable and peaceful re-establishment of David's kingdom. Such ideas derived colour from the fact that in Hezekiah, during whose reign Isaiah and Micah were at the height of their activity, a relatively righteous, able, and upright monarch was seated upon the throne of Judah, and amid the downfall of neighbouring kingdoms Jerusalem still remained comparatively secure.

The advent of Jehovah.—The idea of a Davidic king which dominates the prophets of the pre-Assyrian epoch, runs parallel to another conception which was specially prominent at this time, viz., that of an appearance of Jehovah Himself, to set up His kingdom as personal sovereign in the midst of His chosen people, and as judge and redeemer in Zion. This expected moment of divine self-manifestation is to the prophets a turning-point in human history—the day of judicial intervention, the day of God's decisive act, the day of Jehovah's exaltation. In this conception of the *day of the Lord*, as in that of the Davidic king, the prophets take up a popular cry, but give it their own peculiar turn. The mass of the nation clung with fanatical confidence to the thought of Jehovah's 'day.' They looked forward to it as a supreme object of hope in all times of distress. They assumed that Jehovah's self-manifestation must necessarily end in the discomfiture of Israel's foes. It was, as we have seen, the special task of Amos (v. 18 ff.) to combat this delusion, and to insist that only through the overthrow of the theocracy in its existing state, and the salvation of a mere remnant, would the divine purpose for Israel find accomplishment (Amos ix. 8; cp. Isaiah vi. 10 ff.). Accordingly, from the rise of prophecy until its close in literature of an apocalyptic type, the thought of 'the day of Jehovah'

LIMITATIONS OF PROPHECY

continually recurs. That momentous crisis was to be a day of outward terror; the ordinary course of nature would be violently interrupted; the works of man would be brought low; his loftiness would be humbled to the dust (Isa. ii. 12). It was to inaugurate a process of moral sifting; it was to be a moment of judgment, in which Jehovah would test and refine both the nations of the world and His own people, *by the spirit of judgment and by the spirit of burning* (Isa. iv. 4). On the other hand, however, the day of the Lord was proclaimed by the prophets as an epoch ushering in the age of Messianic blessings. Though the ungodly mass of the people are warned not to wish for a day which to them shall be *darkness and not light* (Amos v. 18), the faithful in Israel are encouraged to look forward to it with confidence and hope. For that day will be one of deliverance and consolation. It will not merely bring terror to the evil; it will be a day of everlasting joy to the righteous, of relief to the oppressed.

Two distinct lines of thought, then, pervade the prophetic writings of this period and colour the vision of the future: (i) the idea of a Davidic king reigning in righteousness over a spiritually renewed Israel, and (ii) that of a self-manifestation of Jehovah as His people's redeemer and king.

Limitations of prophecy.—The prophets do not however attempt to adjust or combine these two parallel lines of prediction. They describe the Messianic deliverance sometimes as the achievement of a Davidic king, sometimes as the outcome of Jehovah's personal advent. The two conceptions are nowhere actually combined in a single divine-human figure. They form continuous and co-existent elements in Messianic prophecy, and meet us again in the writings of Jeremiah and Ezekiel. The last-mentioned prophet places the two ideas in close juxtaposition in his thirty-fourth chapter (vv. 11, 23, 24), where he represents Jehovah Himself as the shepherd of His people, and the Davidic king as a prince ruling in His name.

It should also be noticed that the prophets represent the Messianic kingdom under forms and figures suggested by their present experience. They picture a kingdom of God visibly founded on earth, with Jerusalem for its recognised centre. Thus Isaiah takes as the keynote of his earlier prophecies a prediction, perhaps borrowed from some older prophet, in which Zion's exaltation is described. In the after-days Zion is to be the spiritual metropolis of the world. 'Its spiritual preeminence is represented under the figure of a physical elevation of the temple mount. Thither not Israel only, but the nations of the world, will go up to worship and to learn from Israel's God.'[1] The tendency of later prophetic thought was to revert to this early conception. Thus Ezekiel's book closes with a vision of the temple restored as the earthly dwelling-place of Jehovah in the midst of His people, while the later Isaiah looks for the restoration of Jerusalem in radiant splendour, as the scene of a spiritualised Levitical worship, in which all the nations of the earth are summoned to participate. Once more, in their prediction of future blessings, the prophets know not the time or manner of fulfilment. To them the present and future are contiguous and as yet undistinguished. They generally proclaim salvation as a blessing of the near future; yet the delay of Messianic blessings does not shatter their hope or confidence, mainly because they are so keenly alive to the *conditional character* of Jehovah's word; they teach that impenitence or apostasy on Israel's part necessarily interrupts or postpones the dawn of the Messianic age.

The idea of the Messiah as a Davidic king seems, as we have observed, to culminate during the reign of Hezekiah, and it meets us again in the writings of Jeremiah (xxiii. 3-6, xxxiii. 15), of Ezekiel and of Zechariah. The date of the passage Zech. ix. 10 is very uncertain, but its insertion in the writings of a post-exilic prophecy shows that the hope of earlier times was not materially changed. In this passage Messiah is depicted as entering into Jerusalem in the garb of a prince of peace, *just, and having salvation, lowly, and riding upon an ass and upon a colt, the foal of an ass.* Without the

---

[1] Kirkpatrick, *op. cit.* p. 183.

implements of war He extends His righteous sway. *He shall speak peace unto the heathen, and his dominion shall be from sea even to sea, and from the river even to the ends of the earth.*

Effect of Manasseh's reign.—But the reign of Manasseh not only produced a violent anti-prophetic reaction, during which the active ministry of the prophets was suspended;[1] it gave birth to a consciousness of the distinction between the faithful few, and the ungodly mass of the nation which had fallen away into idolatry and libertinism. The hopes of the future came to be connected no longer with the discredited fortunes of the royal house, but with the constancy of the pious remnant of Israel, which amid circumstances of the utmost discouragement still clung to the hopes, and obeyed the teachings of prophecy. This remnant of the nation became more and more distinctly conscious of Israel's true vocation; but although it set itself with zeal to *seek Jehovah* (Zeph. ii. 3), it nevertheless found itself involved in the overwhelming calamities which after the death of Josiah overtook the Hebrew people. The cataclysm of the exile followed, bringing to the faithful a long period of suffering and probation, during which the Israel of God gradually awoke to the sense of its function as a missionary to the nations. This faithful remnant, in accordance with a characteristic tendency of the Hebrew mind, is individualised as a righteous person who bears the iniquity, even while he fulfils the true destiny of his people. 'In this ideal *servant of Jehovah* are concentrated the scattered characteristics of God's faithful: their spirit of dependence, their patient devotion, their unswerving faithfulness in the fulfilment of vocation, their brave constancy under trial, their meek acceptance of death.'[2]

Isaiah liii.—In the fifty-third chapter of Isaiah we again reach a culminating point in prophecy. The righteous servant of Jehovah is depicted as pouring out his soul unto death, making atonement for the transgressions of

---

[1] Mic. vi. and vii. possibly belong to Manasseh's reign.
[2] *The Doctrine of the Incarnation*, i. 55.

his people, and passing through death to a new and glorified life of fruitfulness and power in which he sees of *the travail of his soul* and is *satisfied*.

The exile thus developed in Israel's consciousness the thought of the mediatorial functions of God's people as embodied in a representative individual. The universalistic ideas of earlier prophecy revived. In Ezekiel Israel is represented as a restored people renewed by the power of Jehovah's Spirit, sanctified by the presence of His sanctuary in their midst, and enjoying under the sway of an upright prince the blessings of righteous government. Israel is contemplated as a priestly people separated from the world by a ring-fence of sacred institutions. But the later Isaiah is full of the thought of the universal mission of His people. He recognises the prophetic and missionary character of Israel—its vocation to be *a light to the Gentiles* (xlix. 6). Zion becomes the spiritual mother of the nations. Thither the Gentiles bring their offerings; the sons of the alien serve her and build up her walls; *the abundance of the sea* is converted to her, *the forces of the Gentiles* minister to her (Isa. lx.-lxii.).

Post-exilic Prophecy.—This sense of the priestly character and office of Jehovah's people may have enhanced the new significance assigned to the priesthood by post-exilic prophecy. In Zechariah's book, Joshua the high-priest stands on a level with Zerubbabel the theocratic prince. The idea of atonement found a fixed outward expression in the ritual of the restored sanctuary. The sense of sin was gradually educated; hopes and anticipations of a spiritual kind were developed. Thus in Psalm cx. is to be found another climax. Zechariah represents the prince and priest as ruling in perfect harmony and even sharing a single throne. *The counsel of peace shall be between them both* (vi. 13). But in Psalm cx. prophecy rises to the thought of a monarch who, as the representative of the priestly nation, himself holds the dignity of the priesthood, being made by the oath of Jehovah *a priest for ever after the order of Melchizedek*. This is the nearest approach we have to a combination of the figure of the suffering servant with that of the Davidic king.

The new Covenant.—The restoration of the temple-worship naturally brought again into prominence the idea of a *covenant* between Jehovah and Israel—an idea which corresponds to that of a people of God charged with a spiritual mission to mankind. The hope of a covenant of grace, under which Jehovah would Himself accomplish what Israel had failed to fulfil, had already appeared in Jeremiah (xxxi. 31 ff.). Jehovah had purposed to make Israel a kingdom of priests and an holy nation, but the only hope of the ideal being realised lay in the free action of Jehovah's grace. The old covenant had failed; it was powerless to secure the obedience it enjoined; it was powerless to remove sin. A new covenant would be characteristic of the Messianic age, in which not merely the outward life, but the heart of Israel was destined to be renewed unto holiness. The law of Jehovah should be written in the heart; each soul should have immediate knowledge of God; above all, the burden of sin and defilement should be finally done away. The conception of a new covenant marks an onward step in Israel's religious education; for it implies that the Messiah was not destined to fulfil the aspirations of national ambition, but to satisfy the yearnings of spiritual need. Moreover, it implies that religion is not merely a matter of national obligation, but a personal and individual relationship with Jehovah. A spiritual religion can no longer be a merely national religion. 'When religion is thus carried back to its deepest centre, to the fellowship of man in his heart with God, the separating limits of the national cults fall away as meaningless; the most inward experience of what is purely human can no longer be a privilege of one people above the others—it must become a thing of the whole of mankind.'[1]

In the post-exilic prophets the interest of prophecy naturally centres in the temple, which is regarded as the scene of a future theophany. The sudden coming of Jehovah to His temple will usher in the age of Messianic blessings. Thither the desirable things of all nations shall be brought; there the deepest yearnings of man's

---

[1] Pfleiderer, *Gifford Lectures*, ii. 51.

heart shall be finally satisfied (Hag. ii. 7-9; Zech. ix. 9). In the book of Malachi the thought of Jehovah's coming is modified in a manner characteristic of the period when the prophet wrote. Jehovah will manifest Himself, but through the mediation of an angel, the minister of His covenant and executor of His righteous judgment. On the other hand, we seem to find after the exile a growing sense of the relation of the Messiah to humanity at large. He is again called *the Branch* (Zech. iii. 8, vi. 12; cp. Jer. xxiii. 5), though he stands in unique relation to Jehovah. In Daniel vii. 13, the expression *one like unto a son of man* does not apparently in its original context denote the Messiah. It seems rather to describe the characteristics of that ideal kingdom of the saints which is destined to supersede the heathen empires founded on brute violence and material force. The Messiah (Dan. ix. 25, 26, *anointed prince*) is regarded as one with the saints of the Most High—their head and representative, exercising the universal dominion bestowed on Israel by Jehovah Himself.

The Post-Canonical Literature.—The general tendency, however, of the later apocalyptic literature is to depict Messiah as a human prince, exalted, majestic, and even divinely endowed, but as one whose victorious sway ministers to the national exaltation of Judaism and of the synagogue. Thus in the apocryphal books, for instance, there is practically no reference to a personal Saviour. Vague hopes of the future glory of Zion, of the conversion of the Gentiles, and of the deliverance of Israel from its heathen foes, are the most prominent elements in the Messianic pictures of these books. It falls however outside the limits of our present task to describe them particularly.[1]

The argument from prophecy when re-stated in the form rendered necessary by our present critical knowledge is very parallel in its results to the modern shape assumed by the argument from design. In both cases

---

[1] For an account of the Messianic expectation in its later stages, see Schürer, *The Jewish History in the time of Christ*, § 29.

the inductive conclusion is drawn, no longer from the narrow field of special cases of correspondence, but from the broad area of prophecy surveyed as a whole. Approaching the Old Testament from the point of view of belief we find a *general* correspondence between fulfilment and prediction sometimes rising to the point of wonderful minuteness. But it is needless to lay stress on special predictions, or to look for particular miracles of foresight where all is divine. A critical study of various Messianic passages shows us that their original application and reference is to events and circumstances of the prophet's own day; but the ultimate reference to Christ is justified by the maxim of 2 Peter i. 20: *No prophecy is of private interpretation.* Scripture is seen to have successive applications corresponding to different stages in the work of God. That which, for instance, was originally spoken of the chosen nation (*e.g.* Hos. xi. 1), found a fresh and ideal fulfilment in Him who embodied in His representative humanity the people from whom as touching the flesh He sprang, and who recapitulated in His own life the experience of all the ancient saints; and that which was truly accomplished in Him necessarily had a mystical reference also to the spiritual *Israel of God* and the Christian Church of which He was the founder and archetype. Finally, the individual Christian, in so far as he realises his union with Christ, discerns in the narrative of Israel's fortunes and in the institutions of its polity and worship, a kind of description, writ large, of his own spiritual course and moral experience.

For what gives prophecy its peculiar character, as at once a message addressed to the present, and a picture of future glory, is the fact of inspiration. The word of God came to the prophets; in prophecy we have a continual forthcoming of that Word who in the Incarnation was *made flesh and dwelt among us.* Prophetism is indeed a kind of continuous miracle, 'a Pentecostal phenomenon' in history. We can only measure its vast significance if we compare the religion of Israel with the rude beliefs and practices of the primitive Semites, or if we contrast the conception of a merciful and righteous God with those different forms of nature-religion which held the ancient world in spiritual thraldom. It was the work of the prophets to declare the 'Name' of God as it gradually unveiled itself to mankind. Through their agency religion altogether changed its character. Ancient religion, in all its different shapes, was at best a mere law of external observances; it neither implied true ideas of the divine nature, nor was it necessarily a factor in the moral progress of mankind. The work of the Hebrew prophets on the other hand, was both to reveal the essential character of God, and to educate the conscience and will of their fellow-men. In proclaiming the supremacy of the law of righteousness and identifying it with the will of Almighty God, they laid the foundations of a universal religion; their teaching contained in germ the *everlasting Gospel* proclaimed by Jesus Christ.

CHRONOLOGICAL TABLE

I.—BEGINNINGS OF PROPHETISM.

Legislation of Moses, cir. 1320.
Samuel, cir. 1040.
DAVID, King, ?1010-978.
SOLOMON, 978-938.

B.C.	Kings of Israel.	Kings of Judah.	General History.	Prophets.
937	Jeroboam I.,	Rehoboam, .		
920	......	Abijam, .		
915	Nadab, .	Asa (917), .		
914	Baasha, .	......		
890	Elah, .	......	......	
889	Zimri, .			
889	Omri, .	......	......	
877	Ahab, .	Jehoshaphat (876).		ELIJAH.
855	Ahaziah, .	......		......
854	Jehoram, .	......	......	......
851	......	Joram, .	......	ELISHA.
843	......	Ahaziah, .	......	......
842	Jehu, .	[Athaliah], .	Israel engaged in disastrous war with SYRIA.	......
836	......	Joash, .	......	......
814	Jehoahaz, .	......		......
797	Jehoash, .	Amaziah (796).	......	......

119

II.—THE ASSYRIAN PERIOD.

B.C.	Kings of Israel.	Kings of Judah.	General History.	Prophets.
781	Jeroboam II.,	......	......	......
777?	......	Uzziah,	......	Amos (cir. 760)
745	......	......	Tiglath-Pileser III. (Pul.) King of Assyria.	760-746
740	Zechariah,	......	......	Hosea (cir. 740). 746-734
...	Shallum,	......	......	......
...	Menahem,	......	......	......
737	Pekahiah,	Jotham (sole ruler).	......	Isaiah (cir. 737). 740-700
735	Pekah,	Ahaz,	Syro-Ephraimitish War.	Micah (cir. 735). 720-700
733	Hoshea,	......	......	......
732	......	......	Fall of Damascus.	......
730	......	Hezekiah,	......	......
727	......	......	Shalmaneser IV.	OBADIAH. 725 or 456
722	Fall of northern Kingdom.	......	Sargon,	......
711	......	......	Siege of Ashdod,	......
705	......	......	Sennacherib,	......
701	......	......	Assyrian Invasion of Phœnicia, Philistia, and Judah.	......
686	......	Manasseh,	......	? Micah, chh. vi., vii.
681	......	......	Esarhaddon,	......
641	......	Amon,	......	......

CHRONOLOGICAL TABLE 121

III.—CHALDEAN PERIOD.

B.C.	Kings of Judah.	General History.	Prophets.
639	Josiah,	……	Jeremiah (627). 626-586
627	……	……	Nahum (?656). 664-612
625	……	*Nabopolassar*, King of Babylon. Inroads of the Scythians (*cir.* 625).	Zephaniah (?625). 625-621
621		……	Discovery of the book of the Law (Deuteronomy).
610	……	……	Habakkuk (?608).-597
608	Jehoahaz,		……
607	……	Fall of Nineveh,	……
604	……	*Nebuchadnezzar.* Battle of Carchemish.	……
597	Jehoiachin, Siege of Jerusalem and first deportation.	……	……
…	Zedekiah,		……
592	……	……	Ezekiel in exile (592-570).
586	Fall of Jerusalem, second deportation.	……	……

IV.—PERIOD OF PERSIAN DOMINATION.

B.C.	General History.	Prophets.
550	*Cyrus*, King of Medes and Persians.	Author of Isaiah xl.-lxvi. (*cir.* 550-538).
538	Fall of Babylon,	……
537	First return of the Jews,	……
521	*Darius I.* (Hystaspes),	……
520-516	Re-building of the Temple,	Haggai and Zechariah (i.-viii.).
485	*Xerxes*,	Obadiah ..725 or 486
465	*Artaxerxes I., Longimanus*,	……
458	Mission of Ezra,	……
445	Nehemiah appointed Governor,	Malachi (*cir.* 440).
433	Second visit of Nehemiah,	……
350	……	?Book of Joel. 536-100

V.—GREEK PERIOD.

B.C.	General History.	Prophets.
333	*Alexander* defeats Darius at Issus,	? Isaiah xxiv.-xxvii.
332	Alexander invades Egypt,	
324	Death of Alexander,	
322	*Ptolemy I.* (Soter), King of Egypt,	
? 315	Seleucus expelled from Babylon by Antigonus,	? Zechariah ix.-xiv.
312	Seleucus recovers Babylon,	
301	Palestine a province of Egypt,	? Book of Jonah. *before .. 612*
280	Antiochus I. of Syria,	
198	Palestine falls to the Seleucidæ,	......
175	Antiochus IV. (Epiphanes), King of Syria.	......
168	Persecution of the Jews by Antiochus IV.	......
166	Judas Maccabæus,	......
165	......	Book of Daniel.

INDEX

Abraham 2 160 - 2000
Ahab, 12.
Amos, 13, 20; book of, 21 ff.; teaching, 23. 760-746
Antiochus, persecution of Jews by, 104.
Apocalyptic writings, 15, 91.
Assyria, 33 ff.

Baalim, 27.
Baal-worship, 12.
Babylon, rise of, 45.
Balaam, prediction of, 108.
Bull-worship, 24, 27.

Canon of Scripture, 2.
Carchemish, battle of, 45.
Covenant, the new, 60, 115 ff.
Cyrus, 71.

Daniel, Book of, 15, 103 ff.
David, reign of, 109.
Davidic king, the, in prophecy, 37, 110.
Day of Jehovah, the, 20, 96, 111.
Deuteronomy, book of, 35, 53, 68.

Edom, 98.
Elijah, 7, 8, 9.
Elisha, 7, 12. 850-800
Ezekiel, 14, 63 ff., 115. 572-570
Ezra, work and mission of, 84 ff.
Exile, the, 62; literary activity during the, 70, 76; return of Jews from, 76, 78.

Gedaliah, 57.

Hagiographa, the, 1.
Habakkuk, 14, 46, 49 ff. 608-597
Hananiah, 57.

Haggai, 14, 78 ff.
Hosea, 13, 24; book of, 25 ff.; religious teaching of, 28 ff. 746-734
Israel, kingdom of, war with Syria, 17; condition in eighth century, 18, 19.
Isaiah, 13, 30; prophecies of, 32 ff.; 740 present book of, 35; theology of, 36 ff.
—— xxiv.-xxvii., author of, 99 ff.
—— xl.-lxvi., author of, 71 ff., 77, 115.
—— liii., teaching of, 75, 114.

Jacob, blessing of, 108.
Jeremiah, 14, 46, 52 ff.; teaching of, 58 ff. 626-586
Jeroboam II., 17.
Jews, condition of, after return from exile, 78, 84.
Joash, 17.
Joel, book of, 15, 95 ff. 836-800
Jonah, book of, 15, 99 ff. before 612
Joshua, the high priest, 79, 114.
Josiah, reformation of, 53 ff.; death of, 55.
Judah, kingdom of, condition in eighth century, 30, 31; history after death of Manasseh, 53.
Judaism, 86.
Judas Maccabæus, 104.

Malachi, book of, 14, 87 ff.
Manasseh, reaction under, 44, 114.
Megiddo, battle of, 55.
Messiah, Messianic hope, 107 ff.
Micah, book of, 13, 38 ff. 720-700

INDEX

Moses, 108, 109.

Nâbhi, Nebîim, meaning of, 4.
Nahum, book of, 14, 45 ff.
Nathan, oracle of (2 Sam. vii. 4 ff.), 109.
Nebuchadnezzar, 56.
Necho II., king of Egypt, 55.
Nehemiah, 2, 86.
Nineveh, fall of, 45.

Obadiah, book of, 15, 61, 97 ff.

Post-canonical literature, 117.
Priesthood and the Prophets, 10.
Prophecy, place of, in Israel's religion, 3; origins of, 6; epochs in history of, 13; false, 39, 57; limitations of, 112; argument from, in present form, 117.
Prophets, 'former' and 'latter,' 1; ranked as canonical scripture, 2, 3; function of, 5; 'schools of,' 8;

relation to nation and king, 9; to priesthood and sacrifice, 10.

Samaria, fall of, 25.
Samuel, work of, 7.
Scythian invasion, the, 45.
'Second Isaiah,' the, teaching of, 71 ff.
Sennacherib, 34.
Servant of Jehovah, the, 74, 75, 114.
Syria, war of, with Israel, 17.
Syro-Ephraimitish war, 32.

Torah, 1.

Universalism in prophecy, 41.
Uzziah, 18.

Zechariah, 14, 80 ff., 115.
—— ix.-xiv., 92 ff.
Zedekiah, 57.
Zephaniah, book of, 14, 46 ff.
Zerubbabel, 79, 115.

www.ingramcontent.com/pod-product-compliance
Lightning Source LLC
Chambersburg PA
CBHW021940160426
43195CB00011B/1168